A 2024 Starting-Point Guide

Lucerne, Switzerland

Plus, the Lake Lucerne Region

Barry Sanders – writing as:

B G Preston

Lucerne, Switzerland

ISBN: 9798854453110

2nd edition – Updated April 2024-ar

Acknowledgements: The author greatly appreciates Sandra's contributions. She provided substantial editorial assistance and took several of the photographs included in this work.

Photography: Photos and maps in the Starting-Point Guides are a mix of those taken by the author and other sources including Shutterstock, Wikimedia, Google Earth, and Google Maps. No photograph in this work should be used without checking with the author first.

Cover photography by Rogue Teacher Photos: www.RogueTeacherPhotos.com

CONTENTS

Preface & Some Suggestions

This Starting-Point guide is intended for travelers who wish to really get to know a city and not just make it one quick stop on a tour through France or Europe. It is oriented around the concept of using Lucerne as a basecamp for several days. This handbook provides guidance on sights both in town and nearby area with the goal of allowing you to have a comprehensive experience of this beautiful city and Lake Lucerne area.

The Ideal Itinerary:

The First Suggestion: If your travel schedule allows **plan on staying at least 3 nights in Lucerne**. Ideally, you will be able to stay as many as five nights.

This is an area with a wonderful variety of sights outside of town. Several days are needed to gain even a good feel for what this area has to offer. You may even want to split your stay with

Lucerne's Chapel Bridge

some nights in Lucerne and one or two nights in a mountain or lakeside village.

The Second Suggestion: Leave one day open and unplanned near the end of your stay. Build in a day in which you have not pre-booked any excursions or planned major activities.

The reason for this is that, once there, you will discover places which you either want to revisit or learn of new places which appeal to you. If you have a full schedule, you will lose this luxury.

If You Only Have One Day

If your schedule only allows you to stay in Lucerne for one full day, there are two very different approaches which you may want to consider, depending on your preferences:

1 – City Option: Just visit the main sights in the heart of Old Town Lucerne and spend time exploring the central shopping area and Chapel Bridge then take a stroll up to view the Lion Monument. Make sure you fit in a fondue meal along the river.

Or

2 – Mountain and City Option: You can get a feel for not only central Lucerne but a neighboring mountain as well. It makes for a full day, but you will obtain a great understanding of the area. Start your day early with a trip up to the top of Mt. Pilatus, have lunch at the mountain resort area, come back down via gondola then bus back into central Lucerne where you can spend the remainder of the day exploring the shopping and restaurant area in the heart of Old Lucerne.

Consider a Travel Pass: If you are likely to visit any area museums, head to the top of a mountain or use local transportation, then you may want to consider acquiring

SWISS TRAVEL PASS

one of several available passes. They can be expensive but can also alleviate some hassle and cost. Chapter 4 outlines the most popular passes in the area.

Visit the Tourist Office:

Lucerne's main Tourist Information Office is conveniently located at street level of the train station. Even if you have done substantial research prior to your trip, the staff here are likely to provide information which was missed.

Website: www.Luzern.com

Services Provided Include:

- <u>Obtain information on available tours</u> and places to visit. Many tours may be booked here.

- <u>Purchase City Passes</u>: The staff will provide details on the pass options available.

- <u>Local transportation assistance</u>. Most European cities such as Lucerne will have excellent transportation systems. In the case of Lucerne, there are also several delightful ferries to help you navigate Lake Lucerne. There is no city tram system here.

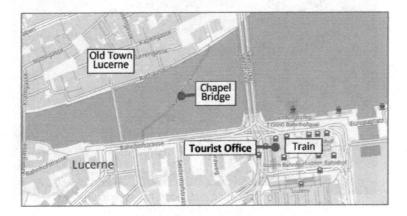

Don't Limit Your Explorations to the City of Lucerne:

Yes, the small city of Lucerne is beautiful, but this is just a small part of what the immediate area has to offer. Use Lucerne as your basecamp but plan on devoting as much time as possible to the varied destinations nearby.

The most obvious choice for exploration is the beautiful mountains which surround you. And, for most visitors, a trip up to at least one of the nearby mountains should be at the top of the list. (See chapter 6 for suggested mountain adventures). Don't limit your explorations to the mountains, however. Consider also exploring the lake area, and perhaps taking a cruise on one of the historic ferries (Chapter 7). There are several attractive towns and villages lining the shore and a day trip to one of them should be on every visitor's itinerary. (Chapter 8, provides guidance on lakeside towns). One fun feature of these towns is that many provide gondola or cog rail travel from the town up to a mountain resort.

Weggis - one of several easy-to-reach towns along Lake Lucerne.

Download Some Apps:

With the incredible array of apps for Apple and Android devices, almost every detail you will need for a great trip is available up to and including where to find public toilets.

Lucerne Specific Apps:

- Lucerne Travel Guide: Good level of details on area attractions and tours. Provided by ETips, a firm which provides similar apps for other cities.

- Audio Tour Luzern: Tour maps and suggested walks on Lucerne/Luzern. Good level of details on area sights along with audio descriptions.

Switzerland Travel and Helpful Information:

- SBB Trains: The Swiss national train system. Schedules, routes, and ability to purchase train tickets.

- Swiss Events: The app provides updated information on thousands of small and large events throughout the country.

The Lucerne Travel Guide App is one of several which can be quite helpful.

- Switzerland Mobility: Details on hiking, biking, and cross-country skiing throughout Switzerland including trail details.

- Swiss Travel Guide: Similar to the SBB Trains app, but broader in that it includes bus, ferry, and train schedules along with details on key attractions.

- Swiss Travel Pass: The perfect app and service to use for travel by almost every mode of transportation in Switzerland. One caution, the pass is expensive.

5

General Travel Apps:[1]

- Rome2Rio: An excellent way to research all travel options including rental cars, trains, flying, ferries, and taxis. The app provides the ability to purchase tickets directly online.

- Trip Advisor: Probably the best overall app for finding details on most hotels, restaurants, excursions, and attractions.

- Flush: A very helpful app which provides guidance on where to find public toilets.

~ ~ ~ ~ ~ ~

---

[1] **General Travel Apps**: There are numerous excellent travel apps to select from. The ones cited here are recommended by the author, but your search for helpful apps should not be limited to this.

1: Lucerne–Gateway to Central Switzerland

Lucerne[2] is located in central Switzerland in the Canton or district of Lucerne at the western end of Lake Lucerne. This is a large town with a population slightly over 80,000, making it the largest town in central Switzerland. The urban area, which comprises nearby towns and villages, has a population of around 220,000.

This is a good basecamp for explorations throughout central Switzerland. Once here, there is enough to offer greatly varying experiences every day for a full week. As outlined in further chapters, there are numerous mountain trips available, lake excursions, and exciting day trips.

Due to its beauty, setting and the array of activities, Lucerne is a popular destination. The town is compact and easy to explore. Many visitors will find that most of the Old Town highlights can easily be visited and explored in one day. Most of

> **Lucerne or Luzern?**
>
> Both spellings are appropriate with "Lucerne" the most common when using English. For simplicity, this guide will stay with default to the Lucerne spelling.

---

[2] **Lucerne vs Lausanne:** Two different cities with similar names. When planning a trip to Lucerne, take care to note that Lausanne is an entirely different city located in the western sector of Switzerland.

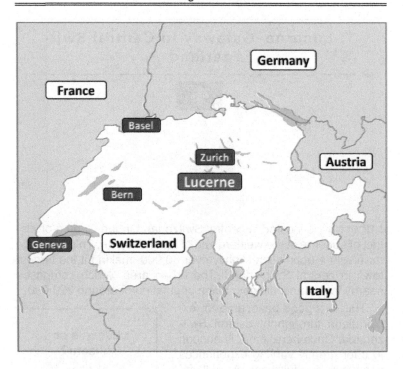

your time will be spent heading out into the country to explore the mountains and lake area.

Visitors to Lucerne are provided with a panorama of magnificent views in almost every direction. The town, which dates to medieval times, was once a fishing village. Today, the Old Town/Altstadt section is set out in a series of charming squares with several impressive churches. The Chapel Bridge, which crosses the Reuss River near Lake Lucerne is the focal point for many visitors and a joy to cross. There is even a gift shop midway across the bridge.

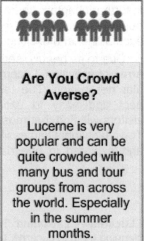

Are You Crowd Averse?

Lucerne is very popular and can be quite crowded with many bus and tour groups from across the world. Especially in the summer months.

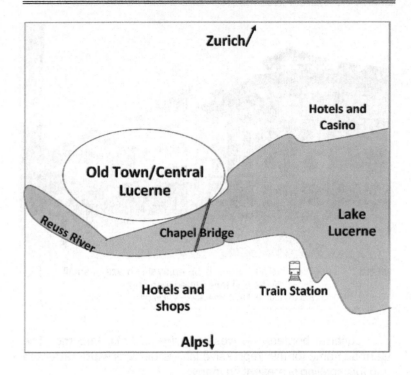

Much of the historic center is car-free, providing enjoyable strolling for visitors. Numerous historical houses line the walks, and the many shops and restaurants invite you to step in and explore or dine. This section of town is where most visitors first go and for good reason. The narrow streets lined with delightful architecture and stores provide enjoyable strolling. Many of the stores are upscale and expensive, but not all, and the budget-conscience visitor will find some stores offering affordable gifts. There is even a quaint gift shop in the center of Chapel Bridge.

Switzerland is divided into four language regions including French and German speaking regions. Lucerne is in the German district. When visiting here, while German is the official language, English is frequently spoken and visitors from English-speaking countries will rarely have a problem in central Lucerne. Language issues may arise when visiting neighboring towns, however.

9

Lucerne's historic center is an enjoyable maze of small plazas and lanes lined with shops.
Photo Source: Matthais Kabel - Wikimedia Commons

Lucerne borders the western edge of Lake Lucerne. The German name for this impressive lake is der Vierwaldstättersee and this spelling is present on many signs around the area. The lake's name means "Lake of the four forested settlements" and is Switzerland's fourth largest lake.

Several notable museums, such as the Swiss Museum of Transport, the Modern Art Museum, and the Rosengart Collection (art museum) are available to visit year-round. With attractions such as the Swiss Chocolate Adventure, there is something here for visitors of every age. See chapter 5 for details on Lucerne's leading attractions.

Accessibility Caution

Areas of Old Town have cobblestone roads which can be problematic to individuals in wheelchairs or scooters.

Delightful views and architecture are everywhere in Lucerne.

For individuals interested in outdoor adventures, there is an extensive array of trails ranging from easy to difficult. Trails can be found leading directly from Lucerne or other trails can be started further up in the mountains. Each of the mountain resorts outlined in chapter 6 have enjoyable trails to explore.

Cars are rarely needed here. The Swiss transportation system is one of the best in the world and every location, ranging from a few blocks away to towns across the lake, are easy to reach. Chapter 7 provides several travel pointers for using Lucerne's ferry system.

Sunday Closures

When planning your visit, it may be helpful to know that many businesses in Lucerne close on Sunday. If you visit on a Sunday, focus on out-of-town activities and not in-town browsing.

Some Interesting Facts about Lucerne:

- The elevation of Lucerne is much lower than its mountain setting would lead most of us to guess. It is only 436 meters above sea level. (1,430 feet).

- The city is bisected by the river Reuss. This is the river which you cross when visiting the Chapel Bridge. The right bank, or northern, side of the river is Lucerne's Old Town.

- The city of Lucerne is spread across 17 municipalities (neighborhoods).

- The name Lucerne comes from the local Benedictine monastery of St. Loedegar which was founded in the 8th century.

- This is the most populated city in central Switzerland and the sixth largest within the country.

- Lucerne is in the German portion of Switzerland. 65 percent of local residents have German heritage and speak German. The next largest group of residents are French who account for 18 percent of the city's population. After this, there is a mix of ethnic groups who speak a variety of languages.

- Within Switzerland the code of CH is used for currency and is the common country code. This code comes from the historic designation of "Confedaratio Helvetico", an earlier political federation. Lucerne was, for a short while, the capital of the Helvetic Republic.

- This was once a walled city. The Museggmauer wall built in the 14th century was designed to protect the city from attackers. Today, parts of the wall still exist along with four of the original towers.

- Lucerne has a world-class concert hall. The KKL Luzern is next to the train station and is an impressive and modern facility to visit.

- During the French Revolution, hundreds of Swiss Guards were massacred. Today, an impressive monument, the _"Lion of Lucerne"_ honors them.

~ ~ ~ ~ ~ ~

2: Traveling to Lucerne

Traveling to Lucerne generally requires a train or bus trip from Zurich, Bern, or Basel. A trip into Lucerne from any of the neighboring cities is easy, scenic, and most routes are short in duration.

Should you choose to drive, this city and its surrounding area are easy to navigate. The streets in and around Lucerne are well laid out and there are parking garages available. If possible, consider not bringing a car as it is not needed here. Should you want to rent or drop off a rental car while in Lucerne, several major auto rental companies have convenient offices. There are some on the outskirts and may require a taxi to or from central Lucerne.

Arriving by Air

Lucerne has an airport but no commercial flights. Most travelers will find it best to fly into Zurich and then travel by train from there to Lucerne.

Trains and buses into the town are frequent and generally convenient to your needs. If you are booking travel to and from Lucerne on your own, use trains if possible. The scenery along the way is beautiful and you can travel in a relaxed mode.

Suggested Website and App: Among the many great transportation websites, the **Rome2rio.com** app is among the best. This service provides side-by-side comparisons for several transportation modes. Tickets may be purchased through this service.

Arriving by Train:

Trains are often the best way to travel to Lucerne and many other cities and towns in the region. The chart on the next page depicts typical travel times to here from major cities nearby.

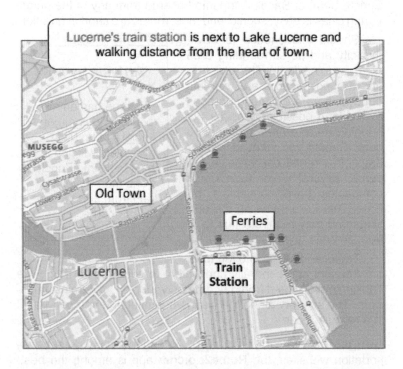

Lucerne's train station is next to Lake Lucerne and walking distance from the heart of town.

Lucerne has one main train station so little confusion will arise as to which station you are arriving at. NOTE: Tickets and routes typically label the town as "Luzern" not Lucerne. Some services such as Rome2rio, label this destination as **"Canton of Lucerne."**

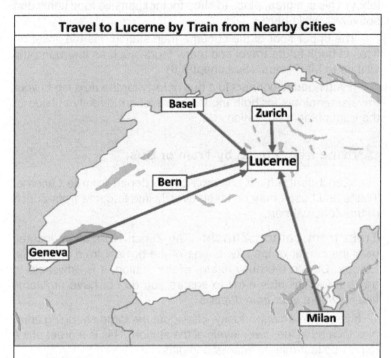

Travel to Lucerne by Train from Nearby Cities

To / From	Typical Time	Trains Per Day
Basil	1 Hour +	10+ Trains
Bern	1 Hour +	10+ Trains
Geneva	3 Hours +	10+ Trains
Milan, Italy	4 Hours +	3 Trains
Zurich	45 Minutes	10+ Trains
Zurich Airport	1 Hr 15 Min	10+ Trains
Some routes require a change of trains midway. Data Source: rome2Rio.com		

This is a midsize but busy station. Of help to many is the large shopping mall on the lower level, just below the main station lobby. This is a great place to shop for inexpensive food items and souvenirs while here.

The upper floor of the Lucerne train station has the ticket offices to book future travel and many tours, such as the round-trip visit up to Mt. Pilatus. (See chapter 6)

If you need to connect to a bus or ferry for the next leg of your travels, terminals for both modes of travel are directly outside of the front of the train station.

Arriving from Zurich by Train or Bus:

Zurich is the most common city to depart from to Lucerne. Trains and buses may be taken directly into Lucerne from Zurich or the Zurich airport.

Train from central Zurich: The Zurich HB station, located near the center of the city, is one of the busiest train stations in Europe. Due to the busy nature of the station, it is advisable to arrive a few minutes early to ensure you do not have problems finding where your train departs.

If you have an opportunity, check out the large shopping complex located in the lower levels of the station. This is a great place to pick up last-minute snacks and gifts.

Numerous trains head to Lucerne from this station each day. The typical travel time is under 1 hour. Not all trains are non-stop, however. Check your booking source such as RailEurope.com or Rome2rio.com to see if your train is nonstop.

Trains from Zurich Airport. The Zurich train station is located in the lower levels of the airport, near the central part of the main terminal. Numerous signs are posted to guide you to this station.

Note: Trains to Lucerne from Zurich airport are not all direct. Some trains do take you directly to Lucerne, but most will require a change in central Zurich. Expect a wait between trains of under twenty minutes, so it is important to head directly to the platform for the Lucerne-bound train once you have arrived at Zurich HB Central.

Check Rome2rio.com, RailEurope.com or similar site to learn in advance if your train trip from the Zurich airport is direct or requires a change in central Zurich.

Bus from Zurich or Zurich Airport: Buses are available from the airport or from central Zurich. The time and funds required are similar to taking the train. When arriving in Lucerne, the buses drop you off just outside the train station.

Buses are not as frequent as trains, so checking their schedule to see how it aligns with your plans or flights is important. Check the following for current bus schedules.

- www.Rome2rio.com,
- www.FlixBus.com, or
- www.BusBud.com.

Switzerland's Name in French and German

When doing your planning you may see variations for Switzerland in formal place names:

French: Suisse

German: Schweiz

~ ~ ~ ~ ~ ~

3: When to Visit Lucerne

Lucerne, and most of Switzerland, have distinct high and low tourist seasons. As a caution, given the popularity of Switzerland for visitors from across the globe, even the "low" seasons are active and buzzing with visitors.

At any part of the year, there is wonderful scenery, great outdoor sports, and activities for all ages. Due to the excellent transportation system in Switzerland, traveling to and from Lucerne or to any of the nearby attractions, even the tallest mountains, is rarely a problem.

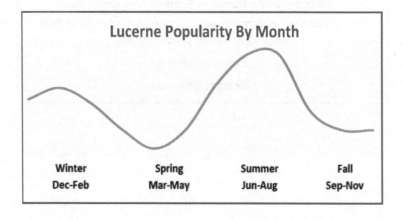

~ ~ ~ ~ ~ ~

Average Lucerne Climate by Month				
Month		**Avg High**	**Avg Low**	**Avg Rain**
Jan	☹	39 F / 4 C	29 F / -2 C	4.3 inches
Feb	☹	42 F / 6 C	29 F / -2 C	2.4 inches
Mar	😐	52 F / 11 C	35 F / 2 C	3 inches
Apr	😐	60 F / 15 C	41 F / 5 C	3.8 inches
May	☺	67 F / 19 C	48 F / 9 C	5.9 inches
Jun	☺	73 F / 23 C	55 F / 13 C	6.5 inches
Jul	😐	77 F / 25 C	58 F / 15 C	6.5 inches
Aug	😐	76 F / 24 C	66 F / 19 C	6.7 inches
Sep	☺	67 F / 20 C	51 F / 11 C	4.3 inches
Oct	😐	58 F / 14 C	44 F / 7 C	3.5 inches
Nov	😐	47 F / 8 C	36 F / 2 C	3.1 inches
Dec	☹	40 F / 5 C	31 F / -1 C	3.1 inches

~ ~ ~ ~ ~ ~

19

Winter:

Positives: Beautiful snow-covered mountains, villages, and scenery in every direction. For individuals interested in winter sports, the array of activities is nearly unending. Enjoying a portion of warm fondue is a treat which can be found in many restaurants across the area.

Numerous events are held in January and February which can add to the fun for many. In December, the Christmas and crafts market opens, adding a lively element to visiting the Old Town.

Crowds are smaller during early December, along with lower hotel prices. This changes noticeably as Christmas approaches and the number of visitors increases.

Negatives: The largest negative for some is the cold and frequent precipitation. Come prepared to walk around on snow and ice and wear warm clothing, especially when visiting the mountains.

Prices from mid-December through February are high as the ski season is in full swing.

Major Winter Festivals:

- **Lucerne Christmas and Crafts Market:** A series of markets, focusing on local crafts. Held from mid-December until Christmas. Numerous local vendors display their crafts in Old Town section of Lucerne. Check out the events section within www.MySwitzerland.com for details.

- **Saint Nikolaus Day:** December 6. A lively celebration of Saint Nikolaus with a torchlight procession in the evening.

- **Lilu – Light Festival:** Mid to late January. Much of Lucerne is lit up and is a beautiful showcase of colorful buildings, especially those which face the river and lake. In the evening, many attractions and streets are illuminated.

- **Valentine's Day:** February 14 is a lively time throughout Switzerland. Flowers will be on display throughout Lucerne and many restaurants will have special menus.

Spring:

Positives: Less crowded than other seasons during March and April and, due to this, hotel prices are often lower than the high Christmas or summer seasons. In May, the crowds start to ramp up along with a corresponding increase in hotel prices.

Winter sports are still available in March, especially at higher altitudes. This can be a great time to get in some skiing without the crowds.

There are beautiful snow-covered hills and mountains that offer wonderful photography opportunities. For individuals who enjoy hiking, late April through May is a great time to explore the lower mountain trails and do so crowd-free.

The weather, especially in April and May, is good and the ability to tour nearby mountains or take lake excursions is generally favorable.

Negatives: Expect snow during March and early April. Rain is frequent in mid-spring, especially in May.

Some tours are not yet open in early Spring, so check ahead with the tour provider to ensure that a desired excursion will be available during your visit.

Summer:

Positives: Summers in Lucerne bring warm weather. Temperatures are typically not hot and the expected highs in the mid-seventies provide for enjoyable explorations.

Even with the warmer days, plan on bringing a jacket if you will be going up any of the nearby mountains. Temperatures at Mt. Titlis, for example, can be in the thirties (f) and snow will likely be present all year.

All non-winter excursions and tours will be available for booking. One caution, this is a busy time so consider booking group excursions in advance.

Mt. Titlis Summer Crowds
Expect crowds when visiting the more popular mountains such as Titlis or Pilatus.

Summer is a great time for hiking and photography. Not all trails are crowded. This is one of the best leisure activities to undertake that can provide scenic beauty without the crowds. If you do not wish to go hiking, every mountain resort has enjoyable overlooks which enable you to appreciate the beautiful scenery.

Negatives: The Summer negatives for Lucerne can be summarized into two words: crowded and expensive.

Lucerne city and several of the mountain attractions are crowded in the Summer. This is understandable given the beauty and charm of the area and that these features attract visitors from all over the world. The crowds are especially problematic when trying to work your way on and off gondolas up to the nearby mountains. One way to reduce the crowds you will encounter is to take excursions early in the day and head up the mountains before most of the bus loads head to the same destination.

The large crowds naturally cause prices for food and hotels to increase. A result of this is that visiting this area can be problematic for individuals without large budgets. See chapter 9 for suggestions on the areas in town which are most likely to provide quality and affordable lodging.

Summer Festivals & Events: [3]

- Blue Balls Festival: Held in July each year, this lively festival is a weeklong celebration of music and art. Numerous musical groups will be on stage, mostly in the evenings, during this 9-day event. For details, check **www.BlueBalls.ch.**

- Lucerne Festival: Each August, and even into September, a series of classical musical concerts is held. The venue for these concerts is the impressive KKL, Lucerne Conference and Concert Center. This impressive building is next to the train station. For details on concerts and ticket availability, check **www.LucerneFestival.ch**

Fall:

Positives: Weather is generally pleasant with cool to warm temperatures. Rain chance is low throughout this season. Most shops and tours will be open through October with some shutting down in November. Hotel rates decrease from their summer highs.

October to early November is a great time to travel up to the mountains as tourist crowds are less than in the Summer and hiking opportunities abound.

Negatives: Negatives are few during this season. There is less snow in the mountains which is a mixed blessing. It improves the ability to explore mountain areas, but there are fewer snow-capped peaks to see.

Some tours and tourist shops will be closed in November.

~ ~ ~ ~ ~ ~

---

[3] **Lucerne Festivals:** Not all festivals and events are cited here. Numerous smaller or specialized events may be found in Lucerne and surrounding towns. For a detailed list, check **www.MySwitzerland.com** or **www.Luzern.com.**

4: City & Area Travel Passes

When visiting Lucerne, there are numerous attractions ranging from small museums to mountain top adventures. Some of these sites can be expensive, especially when traveling with a group or family. If you will be staying in Lucerne for multiple days and plan on visiting several attractions, **acquiring a pass can reduce the cost of visiting Lucerne area attractions**.

Many options for passes in Lucerne and Switzerland are available.

The array of passes can be confusing, and it is easy to purchase an expensive pass which does not fit your needs. To help you select the most appropriate pass, several pass options are detailed here.

Do consider a pass if you are visiting multiple attractions and perhaps using the local transportation system.

Do not purchase a pass if you will only be visiting one or two attractions. The cost of the pass would outweigh any savings incurred.

Pass Comparison					
Pass Type:			Discount Code:		
• LVC = Lucerne Visitor Card • MP = Museum Card • SCP = Swiss Coupon Pass • STP = Swiss Travel Pass • TP = Tell-Pass			• **%** = Reduced Admission to select locations • **F** = Free, no additional charge – for select locations		
Activity	**Pass Type**				
	LVC	**MP**	**SCP**	**STP**	**TP**
Museums	%	F	%	F	%
Restaurants	%		%		
Cable Cars & Gondolas	%		%	F	F
Lake Ferries	%		%	F	F
Transportation - Bus	F			F	F
Transportation - Rail				F	F
Lucerne Wifi	F				
Bicycle, Canoe & other Rentals	%		%		

Lucerne Visitor Card:

Also called the Lucerne Guest Card. This is provided <u>free</u> to overnight guests at most hotels and inns in Lucerne. Discounts to many local establishments are included. The discount varies from 10% to 50% with the most common discount being 20% off the full price.

What it Covers:

- Bus and local train transportation: Free

- Restaurants: Discounts (% varies by restaurant)

- Museums: Discounts (% varies by museum)

- Cable Cars and Mountain Railways: Discounts on selected adventures.

- City Wifi: Free

Cost: No Charge

Limitations: May not be used in conjunction with discounts from other passes. You must be booked into a cooperating Lucerne hotel. (Most hotels do participate)

Website: www.Luzern.com - then go to the page on the Lucerne Visitor Card under the Services section.

How to Obtain: Some hotels will provide the pass and necessary links upon check in. If the hotel does not have this pass information available, then go to the Lucerne Tourism office next to the train station. Once there, show them your check-in documentation and the pass will be provided.

Duration: The pass is valid for the length of your stay in Lucerne.

Lucerne and Swiss Museum Passes:

For individuals who wish to explore multiple museums in Lucerne and perhaps throughout Switzerland. Different geographical coverage versions are available.

Options: You may select a pass which is only for the Lucerne area, or the Swiss Museum Pass covers museums throughout the country.

Acquire this pass ONLY if your focus will be on museums and you are likely to visit multiple museums.

Advantages: The museum passes provide free entry to most of the more popular museums. A few sites, such as the Swiss Museum of Transport, offer pass holders discounts.

Cost:

- Lucerne Museum Card is 39 CHF[4] (Rates are as of April-2024)
- Swiss Museum Pass is 177 CHF (Good for one year)
- Important: This pass is included in the Swiss Travel Pass. If you purchase the Swiss Travel Pass DO NOT also purchase this museum pass.

Website: www.Luzern.com

Where to Buy: Lucerne Museum Passes may be purchased at the Lucerne Tourist Information Office which is located next to the train station. The full Swiss Museum Pass version may be purchased online at **www.MuseumsPass.com**

Swiss Coupon Pass:

This product is provided by Swiss Travel Pass and may be purchased alone or in conjunction with the travel pass. This is a country-wide set of coupons for discounted excursions, restaurants, and travel.

This pass has minimal overlap with the Swiss Travel Pass and provides discounts or free admission to many places not covered by the by the travel pass.

---

[4] **Currency Exchange Rates:** The rates for other currencies such as the U.S Dollar or Pound are generally not shown in this guide due to the changing exchange rates.

As a rough guideline, expect that the US Dollar or UK Pound will be +/- 15% of the Swiss Franc (CHF). Typically, the dollar is worth slightly less than the Swiss Franc and the British Pound will be worth slightly more than a Swiss Franc.

Most coupons are "2 for 1" which, if used by two people, effectively provides a 50% discount. Important, several coupons have a maximum value which may be applied.

When dining, **only one coupon may be used per group**. This limitation means that, for example, if you have a party of two couples, only one coupon may be used for the entire table and not one coupon per couple.

What it Covers: (2 for 1 offers):

- Numerous tourist attractions and museums.
- Guided tours
- Restaurants
- Car Rental via Europcar
- Mountain excursions/Cable Cars/Mountain Railways
- Lake cruise tours
- Motorcycle and bicycle rental

Variations: Available for just one region such as Lucerne or all of Switzerland. If you plan on visiting more than one city in Switzerland, passes are available for 3 or 6 areas. There is also the Swiss Half-Fare Card provided by the same firm.

Advantages: If you have a party of 2 (or multiples of 2 people) and plan on dining at a variety of restaurants and plan on taking multiple excursions, substantial savings can be realized. Do NOT purchase this card if you are likely to use it in only a few places.

Cost: 49 CHF (As of mid-2024). Check the website for all available options and their prices.

How to Obtain: Order online. When you order, you must select either the printed coupon booklet at that time, or the digital version. The printed book is available in several languages. The digital version is only available in English. If you order a printed book, this should be purchased at least 3 weeks in advance to allow it to be mailed to you.

Several firms sell these coupons including (but not limited to):

- Swiss Travel Pass: www.Swiss-Pass.ch
- Switzerland Travel Centre: www.SwitzerlandTravel-Centre.com
- Viator: www.Viator.com
- Trip Advisor: www.TripAdvisor.com.

Swiss Travel Pass: [5]

This popular travel pass allows you to use most of Switzerland's transportation system including trains, bus and ferry systems, and many mountain lifts and gondolas.

When using the Swiss Travel Pass separate reservations are not needed for train tickets, so this adds a significant savings in travel planning.

This pass also includes all museums covered by the Museum Pass. You may take an unlimited number of trips on included modes of transportation.

Cost: Given the many variables, it is best to check the Travel Pass website to determine the cost of a pass which best fits your needs. Some price examples follow.

> The Swiss Travel Pass is available as a printed coupon book or online app.

> **The Swiss Travel Pass is expensive.**
> Only acquire one if you plan on being in Switzerland for at least 3 days and plan on traveling each day.

---

[5] **Swiss Travel Pass vs the Swiss Pass:** The "Swiss Pass" is intended to be used only by Swiss residents. Visitors should consider the "Swiss Travel Pass."

Swiss Travel Pass Price Examples Adult Rates as of April 2024 – Subject to change.				
Days Covered	Standard		Flex Days	
	2nd Class	1st Class	2nd Class	1st Class
3 Days	244 CHF	389 CHF	279 CHF	445 CHF
4 Days	295 CHF	469 CHF	339 CHF	539 CHF
8 Days	419 CHF	665 CHF	439 CHF	697 CHF
15 Days	459 CHF	723 CHF	479 CHF	755 CHF

What it Covers:

- All of Switzerland
- Unlimited train travel
- Unlimited ferry travel
- Unlimited bus travel
- Free or discounted travel on select mountain rail and gondolas.
- 500+ museums, free entry.

> Children travel free when they are with an adult who has a Swiss Travel Pass.

Variations: A complex array of pass options are available.

- <u>Class</u>: Purchase passes for 1st or 2nd class travel.
- <u>Days Covered:</u> purchase passes for 3, 4, 8 or 15 days.
- <u>Flex or standard days: Ticket</u> options cover # of days as a group or flex.
  - o <u>Non-Flex</u>: The # of days covered are in sequence.
  - o <u>Flex,</u> the days purchased, such as 4 days, must be used within 1 month of purchase. This variation is more expensive.

How to Obtain: Order online. Several firms do sell these passes, but it is advised to purchase through the Swiss Pass site. When purchasing through **www.Swiss-Pass.ch**, it is much easier to resolve pass issues while in Switzerland than having to work through an online reseller. Purchase through **www.Swiss-Pass.ch.**

Tell-Pass:

The Tell-Pass is like the Swiss Travel Pass with the one major difference that this pass focuses on central Switzerland. The Swiss Travel Pass covers all of Switzerland.

> A great pass for visitors who will limit their activities to central Switzerland.

This pass also offers unlimited transportation on trains, boats, mountain gondolas, and buses that service this area.

The area defined by this pass includes all of the Lake Lucerne region, west to Interlaken, mountain areas south of Lucerne including Titlis and other popular mountain excursions. It does not cover Zurich, which sits north of Lucerne.

Passes are all issued at the 2nd class travel rate. In many cases, you will be able to upgrade to 1st class on boats or trains when boarding or at the station.

What it Covers:

- Transportation within the region.
- Mountain cable cars and gondolas
- Boat travel on Lake Lucerne
- Limited number of attractions. (Note, this pass does not cover museums as fully as the Swiss Travel Pass. If you are inclined to visit multiple museums, consider acquiring the Museum Pass in addition to this travel pass.

Variations: Like the Swiss Travel Pass, a variety of pass options are available.

- <u>Season:</u> Summer or Winter versions. The Summer version is roughly 50% more expensive per person than the Winter version.

- o Summer: April through October
- o Winter: November through March

- Days Covered: Options include 2, 3, 4, 5 or 10 days. All days must be consecutive and begins the first day the pass is used.

- Age: Separate prices for adults and children. Tickets for children are a fixed price of 30 CHF and do not vary by the number of days involved.

Tell Pass Price Examples (Adult Rates as of April 2024)		
Days Covered	Winter	Summer
2 Days	120 CHF	190 CHF
3 Days	150 CHF	230 CHF
4 Days	170 CHF	250 CHF
5 Days	180 CHF	270 CHF
10 Days	240 CHF	340 CHF

How to Obtain: Order online or at one of several outlets in Lucerne. The website www.TellPass.ch allows you to purchase passes online. It also provides a list of outlets where the pass may be purchased while in the Lucerne area.

~ ~ ~ ~ ~ ~

5: Lucerne City Attractions & Museums
Notable Points of Interest

Lucerne is an enjoyable small city and much of it can be explored on foot. The Old Town and adjoining bridges provide an array of unending photo opportunities. Even if you choose not to explore the nearby mountains or take a boat trip on Lake Lucerne, there is quite a lot to explore right in town.

Lucerne is pedestrian friendly with many enjoyable sights.

There is a bit of a fairy-tale feeling as you explore the numerous narrow stone streets and plazas. It is largely car free which helps visitors who simply want to stroll at their leisure without the worry of being run over. In the heart of town, you will see the historical Old Town Hall which was built in the Italian Renaissance style over 400 years ago. You may also come upon the St. Peter's Chapel which was built in the 12th century.

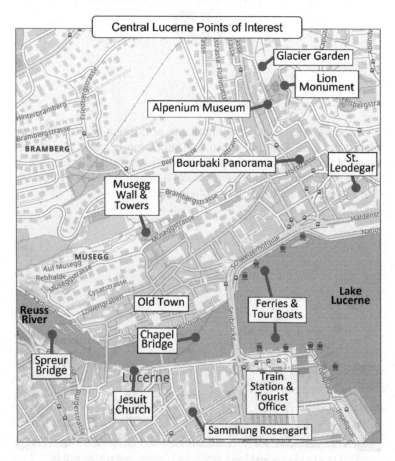

In addition to exploring this historical section with its wonderful architecture, numerous shops and restaurants, Lucerne also offers many attractions ranging from world-class museums to historical treasures. This chapter outlines several of the more popular attractions to consider in town.

Most attractions that have entry fees are covered by one or more of the passes outlined in the previous chapter.

If you are likely to visit several attractions, consider acquiring one of the available passes.

Most of the attractions are within walking distance of Old Town. Only one or two, such as the Swiss Museum of Transport, which is roughly a mile from Old Town, requires transportation such as a bus or taxi. Other popular attractions such as the Lion Monument or Glacier Garden are only a 10 to 15-minute stroll along attractive streets.

Chapel Bridge and Spreuer Bridge:

Two Bridges: The Chapel Bridge, a covered wooden pedestrian bridge, is probably the best known and most iconic site in Lucerne.

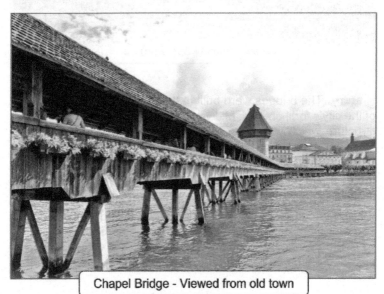

Chapel Bridge - Viewed from old town

What many visitors do not realize is that a companion bridge, the Spreuer Bridge, is just a short distance down river, equally impressive, and far less crowded.

Both bridges cross the Reuss river in a diagonal manner. The bridges connect Old Town at the southern end to the more modern northern area of town. (Also referred to as Lucerne's "Left Bank")

Spreuer Bridge / Spreurbrücke

History: The bridges were built in the 14th century and were part of the city's fortifications. Midway across, each tower sports a side structure which was used as a guard tower in addition to other purposes over time.

Both bridges have suffered disasters such as the fire in 1993 on the Chapel Bridge. As a result, the bridges are now a mix of new structures combined with old woodwork.

Each bridge is adorned with numerous interior paintings, with some of them dating back to the 17th century. Several paintings were redone after the later fires. Explanations of each painting are provided on the bridge.

The Chapel Bridge: Formal name is: "Kapellbrücke." This literally means Chapel Bridge. It is named after the St. Peter's Chapel which is nearby.

- The bridge is 890 ft/270 meters in length.
- This is the oldest wooden covered bridge in Europe.
- In the center of the bridge is a tower which is now a small but appealing gift shop. This tower had once been a water tower. Over time it has even been used as a prison and torture chamber.
- Visitors are not allowed up into the tower.

The Spreur Bridge: Formal name is: "Spreuerbrücke." This name has the unfortunate association with the English word "chaff." Given the downriver position of the bridge, it was the only one in which chaff from the local granary could be dumped into the river below.

- The bridge crosses over the remains of an old mill.
- It was destroyed by a flood in the 16th century and later rebuilt. The rebuild then included a granary.
- The Spreuer Bridge is shorter than the Chapel Bridge. Its length is 266 ft/81 meters.

Unique Attractions in Close Proximity:

Five of Lucerne's popular and unique attractions are very near each other. This allows visitors to easily tour all five without having to charge all over town to do so. Any one of these only entails a short visit and when combined, they make an enjoyable half-day outing.

- Alpineum Museum
- Bourbaki Panorama
- Glacier Garden
- Lion Monument
- St. Leodegar Church

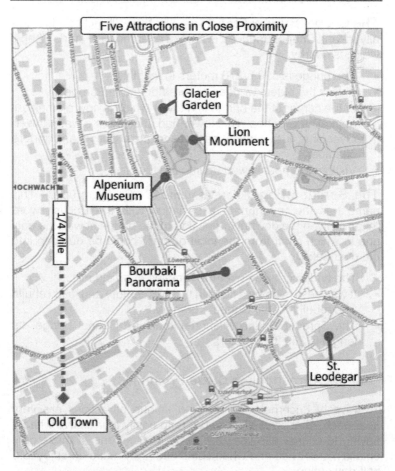

The set of attractions which include a museum, an historical church, a natural formation, a huge historical mural, and an outstanding work of art are easily reached from Old Town by a short walk.

The walk to these attractions is slightly uphill, but most of it can be done on a quiet side street. This is a popular area, and you will find numerous shops, restaurants, and even public toilets to satisfy your needs.

Alpineum Museum / Alpendiorama Luzern

What: A collection of large diorama paintings by Ernst Hodel. The scenes depict the Swiss Alps in an impressive manner. In addition to the paintings, several models of Swiss houses and railway models are on display.

This is an easy museum to tour in under an hour. There is a café on site and restrooms.

Hours: Open Daily (Closed in the winter from November to March)

Website: www.Alpineum.ch

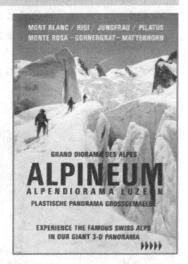

Bourbaki Panorama:

The Bourbaki Panorama - a 360 degree artistic masterpiece.
Photo Source: Wikimedia Commons

What: A Swiss historical monument which utilizes a massive, circular diorama to portray the imprisonment of nearly 90,000 French soldiers who had fled to Switzerland in 1871. Presented in a large round building, you will see a painting over 300' long

(112 meters). The painting and descriptions provide a look into a dark but critical point in Swiss history.

Time to visit this masterpiece is typically less than one hour. There is a restroom and café on site.

Website: www.BourbakiPanorama.ch

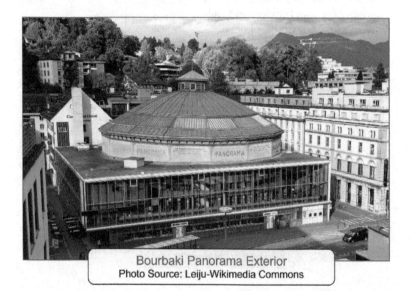

Bourbaki Panorama Exterior
Photo Source: Leiju-Wikimedia Commons

Glacier Garden / Gletschergarten Luzern:

What: Situated next to the Lion Monument is the Glacier Garden. This attraction features glacier potholes which were carved out of rock during the last ice age. When visiting here, you may also see numerous fossils from the area, dating back over twenty million years.

This attraction is a mix of outdoor features and indoor displays and interactive exhibits. Some of the exhibits are geared to children such as the Stone of Time Path and Mirror Maze. There are restrooms on site.

Glacier Garden
Photo Source: Leiju-Wikimedia Commons

Hours: Open Daily Closes at 6PM during the summer months and at 5PM during winter.

Website: www.Gletschergarten.ch

Lion Monument - The Lion of Lucerne:

What: The "Dying Lion of Lucerne" An impressive sculpture carved out of a stone cliff face. It was crafted in the early 19th century in tribute to the many Swiss Guardsmen who died during the French Revolution.

> *"The most mournful and moving piece of stone in the world"*
>
> Mark Twain - 1880

When visiting here, you will first stroll through an attractive small park and come upon a pond which sits at the base of the cliff which holds the large carving. If you are lucky, crowds will be minimal, which would allow you to enjoy this beautiful and often quiet spot which is just a short stroll from the bustle of the tourist area behind you.

Cost: Free and tickets or reservations are not required.

Restrooms: Public restrooms are off to one side of the pond.

The Lion Of Lucerne
Photo Source: A. Savin-Wikimedia Commons

St. Leodegar Church /Hofkirche St. Leodegar:

What: The Church of St. Leodegar is an impressive historical Roman Catholic church located adjacent to Old Town. The current structure was built in the early 17th century on the foundation of a former abbey.

This building is considered to be Switzerland's most important example of a Renaissance period church. The prominent towers are among the few remaining elements after a fire in 1633 destroyed most of the building.

When visiting here, there are several notable features. The pipe organ was begun in 1640 with modifications made in the late 20th century. The organ has over 7,300 pipes, which produce incredible sound if you are lucky enough to be in the church when it is played.

Cost: No fee to enter.

Dining: The church is in a neighborhood with several restaurants.

St. Leodegar Church
Roman Catholic Church

Lucerne Jesuit Church / Jesuitenkirche:

Chapel Bridge

Jesuit Church

Reuss River

Lucerne Jesuit Church
Located near the Chapel Bridge

What: This striking church which sits across the Reuss River from Lucerne's Old Town is the first large Baroque church built in Switzerland. It was built in the late 17th century with some elements not completed until the mid-18th century. It took over what had been a palace for the mayor.

This is a beautiful building inside and out. The interior is striking white with gold trim. The arched ceiling is adorned with impressive art. When built, both German and Italian craftsmen participated, and this is reflected in the architectural elements.

Cost: No fee to enter

Dining: The church is in a neighborhood with several restaurants.

Website: www.JesuitenKirche-Luzern.ch

Musegg Wall and Towers:

What: Also referred to as **"Museggmauer Wall."** A fortification which spans the northern edge of Lucerne's historical center. Currently, the wall and several towers may be toured. A bit of an uphill walk is required to reach the "Wall Trail" as it sits on a slight rise and overlooks the town.

Built in the 15th century, it was an expansion of the city's overall protective system which also includes the Chapel and Spreur Bridges. The wall and its nine towers are 2,600 feet (800 meters) in length.

Not all towers are open to visitors. Some are only available for special events. Check the information board at the base of each tower when visiting.

> This wall provides superb photo opportunities of the town, distant mountains and area.

Musegg Wall & Towers
Photo Source: Lines Voisy - Wikipedia

How to Get Here: The central area and gate of the wall is best reached from the heart of Old Town. This walk will take around 10 minutes and is generally uphill. Look for the street named "Mariahilfgasse" and follow it uphill until it dead ends.

Suggested Duration: Allow roughly two hours to walk up and explore the wall and towers.

Cost: No fee to enter

Dining & Restrooms: No dining or public restroom facilities are available immediately at the wall or in any of the towers.

Seasonal: Closed during winter months.

Website: www.Museggmauer.ch

Museum Sammlung Rosengart:

What: An impressive contemporary and modern art collection situated in the newer section of Lucerne a short walk south of the river. It was created by a private art collector and good friend of Pablo Picasso. The museum houses numerous modern works by such artists as Picasso, Klee, Matisse, and more than twenty others.

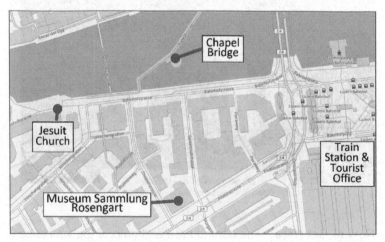

Location: This collection is in a building which was once a large bank. It is located a pleasant three-minute walk from the Chapel Bridge to the north or the train station to the east.

Museum Sammlung Rosengart
Extensive Modern Art Collection

This is a relatively non-tourist part of town where many shops and restaurants may be found. This allows you a relaxing escape from the crowds in the Old Town section of town.

The address is: Pilatusstrasse 10, 6003 Luzern

Cost: Adults 20 CHF, Children 10 CHF.[6] No fee to Swiss and Lucerne Museum Pass holders.

Website: www.Rosengart.ch

---

[6] **Museum Entrance Fees**: All fees shown in this guide are as of mid-2024 and are subject to change.

Swiss Museum of Transport / Verkerhrshaus:

What: Also referred to as **"Verkehrshaus"**, this is a "you shouldn't miss it" attraction if you have interest in any aspect of transportation including air, rail, automotive and water. Exhibits and experiences include both passenger and freight. It is a huge facility on the eastern outskirts of the city and one which has something for individuals of every age.

Swiss Museum of Transport
A Great Family Adventure

Not only is this a transportation museum, but you will also find:

- The "Swiss Chocolate Adventure." Enjoy exhibits and rides detailing how chocolate is made and shipped.

- Hans Enri Museum. Adjacent building displaying works of this noted Swiss artist including a sculpture garden.

- Media World – interactive displays on new and traditional media such as virtual reality and 360 selfies.

- Planetarium – 360-degree astronomy show.

How to Get Here: The museum is around a thirty-minute walk from the heart of Lucerne's Old Town. Given this distance, most individuals will choose one of the enjoyable transportation options available:

- <u>Bus:</u> Included in most city passes this is generally less than a 10 minute ride and several bus routes stop here. Catch one which will stop at "Verkehrshaus-Lido." From there, it is a 5-minute walk to the museum entrance.

- <u>Ferry:</u> One of the more enjoyable ways of traveling to this museum is by ferry. The ferry departs the terminal adjacent to the central train station and, from there, takes you to a dock which is only a short walk to the museum's entrance.

- <u>Train:</u> Trains are also available and may be taken from the central train station. Take the train to the "Luzern Verkehrshaus" station which is a short walk to the museum's entrance. Trains depart hourly.

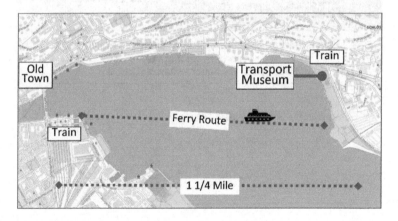

Suggested Duration: Allow for a minimum of a half-day to see most of this large facility.

Restaurant: Full-service and self-service restaurants are on site.

Hours: Open every day with start time at 10AM. It closes at 6PM in the summer months and 5PM during the winter.

Cost: Discounted (not free) if you have a Swiss Travel Pass. Normal rates are variable depending on which areas of this museum you wish to visit. Check the website and the admission page for details. Several rate options are available.

This is a large facility with many aircraft, vehicles and train cars on display.
Photo Source: Ank Kumar - Wikimedia Commons

Website: www.Verkehrshaus.ch

~ ~ ~ ~ ~ ~

6: Mountain Adventures

Explore an Array of Mountain-Top Retreats

Every visit to Lucerne should include a trip up to the mountains. These beautiful peaks call out to you and the Swiss have made traveling to them a joy.

The number of mountains to explore in central Switzerland is nearly unlimited and it could take a book far larger than this to detail them all. Listed here is a mix of some of the more popular mountains along with several more low-key opportunities.

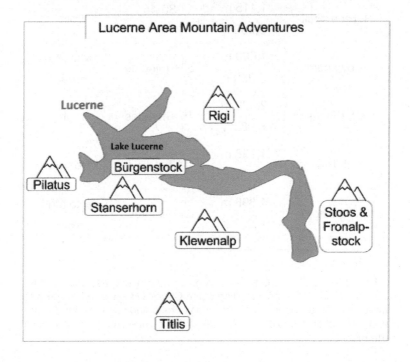

Lucerne Area Mountain Adventures

Lucerne

Rigi

Lake Lucerne

Bürgenstock

Pilatus

Stanserhorn

Klewenalp

Stoos & Fronalp-stock

Titlis

It is natural to want to head out to the taller mountains such as Mt. Titlis but there is a downside to this as you will be far from the only person doing so. Consider also going to some of the closer lower-level and more family-friendly resorts and mountain villages. It is these less prominent destinations which can provide a delightful day along with many opportunities for hiking and great photography.

This guide details seven of the many mountain destinations. All are within easy reach of central Lucerne and none of these locations require travel by car.

7 Mountain Adventures to Consider			
Destination	Altitude	Travel Time to Base[7]	Crowd Potential
Bürgenstock	1,115 m 3,658 ft	30-45 minutes	Low
Klewenalp	1,600 m 5,250 ft	50+ minutes	Low to Moderate
Mt. Pilatus	2,128 m 6,983 ft	15+ minutes	High
Mt. Rigi	1,798 m 5,897 ft	1 hour +	Moderate
Stanserhorn	1,898 m 6,227 ft	20 minutes	Low to Moderate

[7] **Travel Time:** Travel times depicted here are averages which use the Lucerne train station as a starting point. Check **www.Rome2rio.com** for travel time for all modes of travel from your starting point to your destination. Travel time depicted here does NOT include time up to and down the mountain.

7 Mountain Adventures to Consider			
Destination	**Altitude**	**Travel Time to Base[7]**	**Crowd Potential**
Stoos & Fronalpstock	1,921 m 6,302 ft	1 hour +	Moderate
Titlis	3,238 m 10,623 ft	45 minutes	High to Extreme

Lucerne is within sight of many mountains, such as Mt. Rigi shown here.

Cost: All mountain adventures in Switzerland are expensive. This cost can often be reduced with the pre-purchase of local passes such as the Swiss Travel Pass IF you plan on visiting multiple locations. When looking into costs for each of these trips, check to see if they accept the pass you will be purchasing and the level of discount provided.

Bürgenstock:

Bürgenstock Fact Sheet	
Altitude	1,115 m / 3,658 ft
Travel Time from Lucerne	• Ferry: 20-30 minutes • Bus: 40 minutes • Driving: 30 minutes • Train: Not convenient
Town at Base	Stansstad (There is no town immediately at the base)
Ferry Stop at Base	Kehrsiten-Bürgenstock
How to get to Top	Funicular from ferry dock If you are driving take the road up to the resort and bypass the funicular.
Crowd Potential	• Low. Even given the several hotels, this is not one of the top sights which tourists flock to.
Travel Passes Accepted:	• Swiss Travel Pass • Swiss Half-Fare Card • Tell-Pass • Eurail Global Pass
Facilities at Top	• Resort complex with hotels, spa, restaurants, and shops. • Hammetschwand Lift to lookout.
Spring/Summer/Fall Activities	• Hiking – numerous trails • Mountain Biking
Website	**www.BurgenstockResort.com**

This lower elevation destination provides a pleasant mix of upscale resort complex along with a variety of outdoor experiences. Do not let the fact that Bürgenstock is referred to as an upscale resort deter you. It is both a resort and a great place to explore. If your budget allows you the opportunity to stay here, then definitely consider it.

The Bürgenstock Resort

Individuals and families will find a location with incredible views of Lake Lucerne and delightful family-friendly trails. In general, it is not overly crowded and can be a great place to relax and explore.

One unique attraction here is the **Hammetschwand Lift**. This outdoor elevator, Europe's tallest, takes you up to the viewpoint at the top of Bürgenstock. There is an additional fee to ride the elevator.

Neither the elevator nor any of the many trails are restricted to resort guests. The Cliff Path is one of the more popular trails.

Getting Here: This is a case where simply traveling to this hilltop resort is much of the fun. It can be reached by driving, ferry, or bus. The train does not travel directly to here.

Bürgenstock's Hammetschwand Lift

Klewenalp:

Cable Car up to Klewenalp
The longest ride in central Switzerland

Klewenalp Fact Sheet	
Altitude	1,600 m / 5,250 ft
Travel Time from Lucerne	• Ferry: 1hr+ • Bus-Train Combo: 50 minutes • Driving: 20 Minutes
Town at Base	Beckenried
Ferry Stop at Base	Beckenried
How to get to Top	Cable Car. A 5-minute walk from the ferry terminal.
Crowd Potential	• Winter: This is a popular ski area and can be crowded. • Spring-Summer-Fall: Minimal crowds. You can often explore trails without many others around.
Travel Passes Accepted	• Swiss Travel Pass • Tell-Pass
Facilities at Top	• Village with church, restaurant, and small chalets. • Numerous chair lifts.
Winter Activities	• Downhill skiing with slopes ranging from beginner to moderate. • Nordic (Cross-Country) Skiing with numerous trails. • Ski school • Tobogganing
Spring/Summer/Fall Activities	• Hiking – numerous trails • Mountain biking and scooters • Zipline
Website	www.Klewenalp.ch

Klewenalp is an excellent destination for easy hikes with friends and family.

Klewenalp and the neighboring village of Stockhütte provide a vastly different experience from Bürgenstock. This is a destination geared primarily to individuals who wish to enjoy nature and participate in winter and summer outdoor activities.

Situated at 5,250' elevation, this ski area provides a full array of winter sports activities. During the mid-Spring through Fall months visitors will find a relaxed location with wonderful photo opportunities and many trails to hike or bike. The views from here down to Lake Lucerne are excellent.

This is not a place to visit in hopes of finding numerous gift shops. This is, however, a site to visit when you want to experience a low-key Swiss mountain village and recreation area.

Getting Here: The base of the mountain can easily be reached by car, ferry or bus and train combination. Most individuals will choose to travel up the hill on the cable car from the village of Beckenried. An alternative is to take a lift from the village of Stockhütte. Given the many travel alternatives, it is generally best to check with online services such as Rome2rio.com to determine which travel choice fits you best.

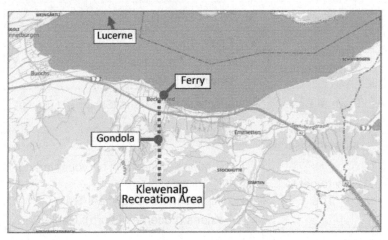

Mt. Pilatus:

Mt. Pilatus as viewed from Lucerne
Photo Source: Liridon - Wikimedia Commons

Mt. Pilatus Fact Sheet	
Altitude	2,128 m / 6,983 ft
Travel Time from Lucerne	<ul><li>Ferry: 1hr+</li><li>Train: 17 minutes</li><li>Driving: 15 Minutes</li></ul>
Town at Base	Alpnachstad or Kriens (Suburb of Lucerne)
Ferry & Train stop at Base	Alpnachstad
How to get to Top	Two options, depending on your starting point:<ul><li>Alpnachstad: Cogwheel Train</li><li>Kriens (Lucerne suburb): Cable Car</li></ul>
Crowd Potential	**High**. Mt. Pilatus is a popular tourist and group tour destination and there is not much room for the crowds to disperse at the top.
Travel Passes Accepted	<ul><li>Swiss Travel Pass</li><li>Swiss Half-Fare Card</li><li>Tell-Pass</li><li>Eurail Global Pass</li></ul>
Facilities at Top	<ul><li>Small hotel with restaurant.</li><li>Hiking Trails</li><li>Scenic Overlook</li><li>Shops</li><li>Restaurant and snack bar</li><li>Astronomy evenings</li><li>Hang Gliding</li></ul>
Website	**www.Pilatus.ch**

A ride up to Mt. Pilatus on the cogwheel train offers dramatic views.

This is a popular destination for many good reasons. The trip, which has several alternatives, is enjoyable, the facilities are modern, and views of the valley, lake and distant peaks are spectacular. The altitude of nearly 7,000 feet is more than enough to give you the feeling of being high up in the mountains while, at the same time, it is not overly cold or up in the clouds. Photography opportunities when visiting here are top notch and great shots can be taken in almost every direction.

Mt. Pilatus
Alpenhorn players entertaining visitors on Pilatus.

The Mt. Pilatus visitor center, hotel and cogwheel train terminal.
Photo Source: Zeledi - Wikimedia Commons

The Pilatus Golden Round Trip and Silver Round Trip:
References to Pilatus's Golden or Silver round trips are frequent

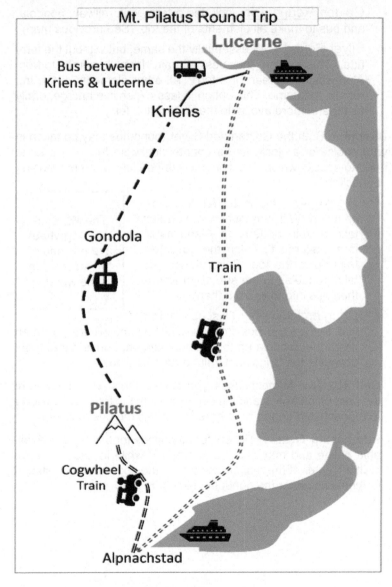

and can be confusing. In essence, this is describing two different ways of planning your trip up to and down from the mountain.

- Golden Round Trip: includes a ferry, cog railway, gondola, and bus to make all elements of the trip. (See previous map)

- Silver Round Trip: essentially the same, but without the ferry ride. This option includes a train from Lucerne to/from Alpnachstad instead of a ferry. All other elements of the trip remain the same. This option is less expensive and generally faster and more available than taking the ferry.

Direction: Both the Golden and Silver roundtrips may be taken in your choice of a clockwise or counterclockwise trip. There is no need to specify which direction you are heading when purchasing your ticket.

- Clockwise: This is by far the most common. With this direction, you first take a train or ferry to Alpnachstad from Lucerne to catch the cogwheel train up to the top. Going down, you take gondolas to the suburb of Kriens then bus into town from there.

> The **Mt. Pilatus Cogwheel Train** is one of the steepest in the world.

- Counterclockwise: This option has you first take a bus from central Lucerne where you then catch the gondola up to the mountain and, once done, head down via the Cogwheel train to Alpnachstad.

Getting Here: In most cases, you will want to start your trip from the area of the train station in Lucerne. Both the train and the ferry to Alpnachstad depart from here as well as the bus to Kriens.

Purchasing Tickets: Tickets for all options for this trip are available online and may also be purchased while in Lucerne from: Visitor Center at the main train station, the cogwheel train station in Alpnachstad, or the gondola office at Kriens.

~ ~ ~ ~ ~ ~

Mt. Rigi:

The Mt. Rigi Cogwheel Train with Lucerne in the distance.

Mt. Rigi Fact Sheet	
Altitude	1,798 m / 5,897ft
Town at Base	Three Options: • Arth-Goldau. Reach by train or bus. Each one takes around 40 minutes. • Vitznau. Reach by ferry, bus, or train-bus combo. Each mode of travel is roughly 1 hour each way. • Weggis: Reach by ferry, bus, or train-bus combo. All travel options are slightly under 1-hour each way.

Mt. Rigi Fact Sheet	
How to get to Top	From: • <u>Arth-Goldau</u>. Cog rail train • <u>Vitznau.</u> Cog rail train. • <u>Weggis</u>: Gondola part way then cog rail train to top. (Note there is an uphill 10+ minute walk from the ferry terminal to the gondola station in Weggis.)
Crowd Potential	• <u>Winter:</u> Moderate. This is a snow activity area and is a draw to many. The large area and variety of options helps in reducing crowds in one spot. • <u>Spring-Summer-Fall:</u> Moderate. While popular, there is a lot of room to spread out up on this low mountain and get away from the hubs of activity.
Travel Passes Accepted	• Swiss Travel Pass • Swiss Half Fare Card • Tell-Pass. • Eurail Global Pass
Facilities at Top	• Overlooks • Numerous trails • Hotel and restaurants • Restrooms • Snack bar
Winter Activities	• Sledding courses • Downhill and Nordic (Cross-Country) skiing • Snowshoe hiking • Ski school

Mt. Rigi Fact Sheet	
Spring/Summer/Fall Activities	• Hiking – numerous trails • Mountain biking and scooters
Website	**www.Rigi.ch**

Mt. Rigi
Alpine meadows with views in all directions.

Mount Rigi is the only mountain adventure listed in this guide which is north of Lake Lucerne. Rigi is a popular destination with an enjoyable journey to reach it. A visit here provides views of lakes and mountains in every direction. Once you reach Mount Rigi via one of the cog rail options, you can then take an easy walk further uphill to Rigi Klum which has a 360-degree lookout. Mount Rigi provides visitors with an open expanse of meadows and trails. You may even find small herds of cattle with their cow bells roaming nearby.

The Rigi cog rail is Europe's oldest mountain railway and offers more than one way to reach the top. Many individuals find benefit in approaching the top from one direction and then heading down by another.

Mount Rigi's facilities are spread out, providing visitors with ample opportunity to explore the trails and numerous overlooks. Facilities include several places to eat along with hilltop hotels. During the winter, there is just about every type of snow sport imaginable.

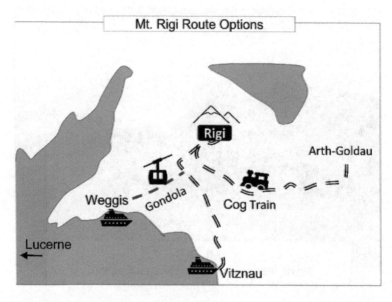

Getting Here: The previous chart shows several travel options. At first, this may seem confusing, and concern may arise regarding which path to take. Do not let this array of travel choices concern you. There is no bad option here. You can easily select a mode of travel which fits your preferences. One caution: If you choose the route via Weggis, the gondola station is a 10–15-minute uphill walk from the ferry terminal. This may be problematic for some individuals. Taxis may be available, but you cannot be 100% certain of their availability.

Suggested Route: First travel via ferry from Lucerne to Vitznau. Once in Vitznau, the cogwheel train departs from the same terminal as the ferry. Take the train to the top. When returning, take the same cogwheel ONLY part-way, down to "Rigi Kaltbad." From Rigi Kaltbad, take the gondola to Weggis where you then walk (or taxi) down to the ferry terminal. The final suggested leg is to take the ferry from Weggis back to Lucerne.

Mt. Stanserhorn:

The Stanserhorn Mountaintop Retreat
Photo Source - Fly01 - Wikimedia Commons

Mt. Stanserhorn Fact Sheet	
Altitude	1,788 m / 6,227 ft
Town at Base	Stans
How to get to Top	From Stans, take a combination of funicular then modern cable car to the top.

Mt. Stanserhorn Fact Sheet	
Crowd Potential	• <u>Winter:</u> Low • <u>Spring-Summer-Fall</u>: Moderate
Travel Passes Accepted	• Swiss Travel Pass • Swiss Half Fare Card • Tell-Pass. • Eurail Global Pass
Facilities at Top	• Overlooks • Numerous trails • Restaurant – including rotating dining area inside the building. • Snack bar
Website	**www.Stanserhorn.ch**

People riding on top of the gondola for an excellent open-air photo op and experience.

Stanserhorn CabriO Gondola
Ride the unique, open-top, gondola up to the top.

Stanserhorn is another peak near Lucerne which provides an enjoyable day of traveling up to a great viewpoint. The trip up to the top includes a combination of an historical funicular then a modern two-story gondola. The gondola allows visitors to ride in the open top deck for a unique treat. The gondola goes by the unique name of CabriO.

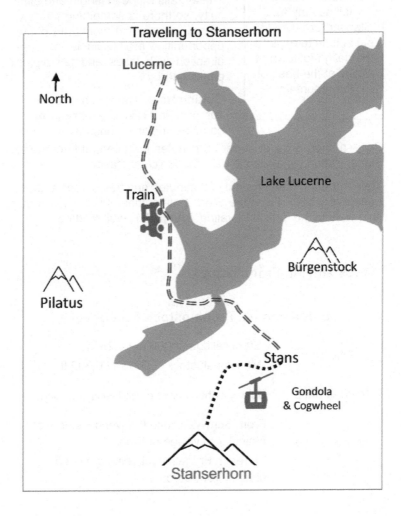

Once at the top, there is a large facility which includes dining both indoors and at a large outside plaza. The indoor restaurant rotates, providing an ever-changing view.

Consider making a full day trip to Stanserhorn by adding in time to explore the delightful town of Stans at the base of the mountain.

Several trails lead out from the restaurant and gondola building. These trails range in length and difficulty, so there is something for everybody. Views and wonderful photo opportunities are available in every direction with lakes and tall alpine peaks nearby.

Getting Here: Travel is best done by car or train. Taking a ferry is more complex and time consuming.

Car – a short drive of under 20 minutes from central Lucerne to Stans. Parking is available near the funicular station.

Train – the trip takes roughly 20 minutes and trains depart about twice every hour. From the Stans train station, it is a short 5-minute walk to the funicular station. The path is well marked.

Stoos and Mt. Fronalpstock:

Stoos and Mt. Fronalpstock Fact Sheet	
Altitude	Stoos village: 1,300 m / 4,265 ft Mt. Fronalpstock: 1,921 m / 6,302 ft
Town at Base	Schwyz (then bus or car to funicular station)
How to get to Top	From Schwyz – take the world's steepest funicular to village of Stoos. To reach Fronalpstock, hike or take a chairlift from Stoos.

Stoos and Mt. Fronalpstock Fact Sheet

Crowd Potential	• Winter - Low • Spring-Summer-Fall-Moderate crowds
Travel Passes Accepted	• Swiss Travel Pass • Swiss Half Fare Card • Tell-Pass.
Facilities at Top	• Overlooks • Restaurants • Chair lifts • Attractive village with hotels
Website	**www.Stoos-Muotatal.ch**

Stoos Village
An enjoyable array of chalets, inns and trails to explore.
Photo Source - Badener - Wikimedia Commons

Stoos (a mountain village) and adjacent Mt. Fronalpstock are on the eastern shore of Lake Lucerne. A trip here provides a number of fascinating experiences.

The Steepest Funicular in the World. Just opened in late 2017. This funicular has rotating cars which adjust as the incline changes. Stoos mountain village is small but scenic at the top of the funicular. The Swiss village is in stark contrast to the ultramodern funicular. The buildings and village areas are spread out, so some walking is necessary to explore it.

The cars on the Stoosbahn funicular rotate as the degree of climb changes.

The Stoosbahn
World's steepest funicular.
Photo Source - S. Gottraux - Wikimedia Commons

There are numerous trails for summer and winter activities. The various trails include everything from mountain meadows to exhilarating hillside walks.

If you come in the winter, a full array of winter activities awaits including downhill and cross-country trails for many different skill levels.

The mountain peak of Fronalpstock overlooks the village and is easy to reach by chairlift from Stoos. Or, if you prefer, take a

30-minute scenic hike in one direction. At the top of Fronalpstock, there is a restaurant and several overlooks with incredible scenery of the lake and towns below and the peaks in the distance.

This is a full-day trip from Lucerne, especially if you choose to take the ferry. The trip to and from provides wonderful scenery. You will encounter several attractive towns along the way and each phase of getting from the town of Schwyz up to Stoos and Fronalpstock is a delight.

Getting Here: As with most destinations in the area, you have several travel choices. The funicular station for the Stoosbahn is slightly outside of the town of Schwyz, so getting to the station requires a bus ride to finish the trip, unless you have your own car.

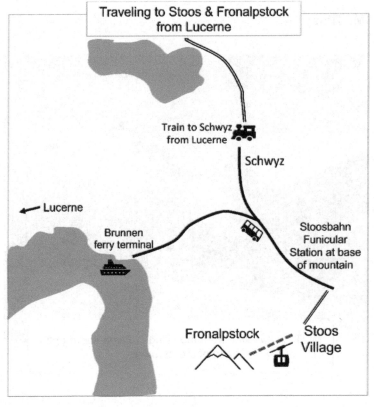

Traveling to Stoos & Fronalpstock from Lucerne

Train to Schwyz from Lucerne

Schwyz

Lucerne

Brunnen ferry terminal

Stoosbahn Funicular Station at base of mountain

Fronalpstock

Stoos Village

When traveling to Stoos from Lucerne, the best options are either a rental car or a train-bus combo. This area can also be reached by taking a ferry to Brunnen and then finishing the trip by bus to the Stoosbahn station. This is not advised as the time commitment each way can be substantial.

Train-Bus Combo: Take the train from Lucerne to Schwyz then catch a bus at the station to finish the journey to the Stoosbahn funicular station. Total travel time each way will be roughly 1hr and 20 minutes. Trains leave frequently from Lucerne. Making connections between the train and bus is rarely a problem and signage is clear.

Mt Titlis:

Mt. Titlis - viewed from the village of Engelberg at the base of the mountain.

Mt. Titlis Fact Sheet

Altitude	3,238 m / 10,623 ft
Town at Base	Engleberg – an easy train trip from Lucerne.
How to get to Top	From Engleberg, it is a short distance to the gondola station. Buses are readily available at no charge or take a pleasant 10-minute walk. Once on the gondola, there is a change midway to the "Rotair," a large rotating car.
Crowd Potential	• Winter and Fall - High • Spring-Summer - **Extreme**
Travel Passes Accepted	• Swiss Travel Pass • Swiss Half Fare Card • Tell-Pass.
Facilities at Top	• Overlooks • Restaurant and snack bar • Cliff Walk • Ice Tunnel/Glacier Cave • Ice Flyer chair lift. • Snow Park.
Spring/Summer/Fall Activities	• Hiking • Ice Flyer Chair Lift • At mid-point, rent a scooter to finish your downhill journey.
Website	**www.Titlis.ch**

A visit to Mt. Titlis provides for a variety of incredible experiences and views.
Photo Source: Ank Kumar - Wikimedia Commons

A visit to Mount Titlis is by far the most dramatic and highest of the seven mountain adventures cited in this guide. It is an easy trip south from Lucerne and has much to offer once there. Even if you do not travel up the mountain, the village of Engleberg is an attractive town to explore and there are other ski lifts which also depart from here.

Visiting here can be a mixed experience. On the positive side, the trip up and down is exhilarating and the views from the top are postcard perfect. These views and the spectacular nature of the peak are drivers for the biggest negative which is crowding.

This is a very popular place. Simply viewing the Gondola station parking lot crowded with tour buses is a clue that you will be far from the only person to visit here. When at the top, which is a treat, be prepared to find yourself surrounded by large, jostling crowds from a mix of cultures. Also be aware that you may be jammed into a gondola with many others which can reduce how fun the journey is.

> **Low Temp Caution**
>
> Due to the elevation, it is almost always cold up here, even on warm summer days. Bring a jacket!

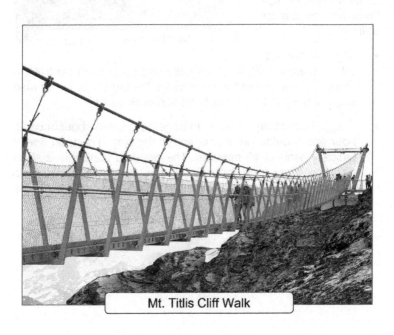

Mt. Titlis Cliff Walk

Several unique features may be found at the top. This includes the Cliff Walk, an open span with wonderful views and a manmade cave through glacier ice. There is also an "Ice Flyer" chairlift which whisks visitors to a glacier park.

Getting Here: This is an easy and relaxing trip from Lucerne. The most common travel options are by car or train.

Mt. Titlis Gondola Station

- <u>Car:</u> A car trip will take around 30 to 40 minutes each way from central Lucerne. This mode of travel provides the benefit of being able to go directly to the gondola station parking lot.

- <u>Train:</u> Trains from Lucerne to Engelberg leave about once an hour and provide great scenery all the way. The train ride is typically around 45 minutes. The gondola station is a short distance away from the train station. Buses to the gondola station are generally available or you can take a pleasant walk to there.

~ ~ ~ ~ ~

7: Lake Lucerne Ferries

Lake Lucerne is a delight to view and calls out to be explored. The exploration is all the more intriguing given the lake's complex shape which includes multiple arms and several small rivers feeding into it. On the western edge, the lake's waters feed into the Reuss River which passes through the heart of Lucerne.

A delightful variety of ferries travel on Lake Lucerne.

The lake is beautiful when seen from the town of Lucerne and for many individuals this will be enough. If your schedule allows, take time to explore the lake region further as these adventures beyond the town are always rewarding. Traveling this lake area, by ferry, train, or car provides visitors with an ever-changing landscape of hills with farms, snowcapped mountains, quaint villages, and charming lakeside towns.

Covering over 44 square miles, the shores of the lake often rise steeply with hills and tall mountains in every direction. Lake Lucerne's German name "Vierwaldstättersee" means "Lake of four forested settlements." These settlements are four of Switzerland's cantons which includes the canton of Luzern.

Most of the villages and towns bordering the lake are serviced by the excellent area transportation system. In almost every case, there are multiple modes of transportation leading to them.

In the previous chapter on mountain adventures, directions often provided guidance to travel to one of these lake towns to board either a gondola or cogwheel train up to the mountain.

Consider not only just passing through these delightful towns but adding in one as a full day trip. The following chapter details several towns which are fun to explore.

Lake Lucerne Ferry Website

Check out **www.LakeLucerne.ch**. This website provides comprehensive information on every aspect of this ferry system and tickets may be purchased here.

You may also purchase mountain excursions and culinary cruises on this website.

Traveling by Ferry:

Traveling by ferry is probably the best way to experience this beautiful lake and area. There is an extensive ferry system on the lake which serves dozens of communities. In addition, several round-trip excursions are available. Many of the towns and villages, especially along the western sections of the lake, are easily reached from Lucerne and may be visited in one day.

There are over a dozen ferries which actively service the area. Most of these ferries are only for passengers.

One ferry line does take both people and autos. It crosses the middle of the lake between Gersau and Beckenried.

When deciding to travel by ferry to a lakeside town, take care not to simply pick a destination at random. Several of the ferry stops do not provide a full array of facilities for visitors as the ferry stops are there primarily to help local citizens come and go.

How to Use the Ferry System:

Whenever a transportation system is used by a visitor for the first time, there is understandable trepidation regarding various elements of the process. With the best of systems, there are always unknowns. The good news with almost every mode of transportation in Switzerland is the Swiss have gone out of their way to simplify things.

The following pointers will help to understand how this charming fleet of ferries operate.

The ferry terminals at several lakeside towns connect directly to local transportation.

Departing Lucerne: Most ferries depart from the main ferry terminal at "Pier 1" which is immediately across from the train station. This location is within walking distance of most of central Lucerne and several bus lines travel here as well. A few specialty routes, such as the catamaran ferry to Bürgenstock, leave from Pier 2 which is a short walk east of the station and across from the large KKL building.

Lake Lucerne Ferries
A mix of classic and modern vessels.

Ticket Options: Ferry tickets, for rides to nearby towns, are available in several ways including: Individual trip tickets, day passes or combination tickets that combine a ferry trip with gondola or cogwheel train.[8]

- <u>Individual Trip Tickets</u>. Buy one-way or round-trip tickets to a specific destination. Prices vary depending on your destination and savings are incurred when a round-trip ticket is

---

[8] **Ticket Prices:** This guide does not cite the cost for tickets for ferries and most transportation for the simple reason that it can and does change. For current ferry rates, check **Shop.LakeLucerne.ch** – this site provides current rates and enables you to purchase tickets prior to your trip.

purchased vs. one-way. If you book via the website, you must know the name of the destination town. No prompts or lists are provided.

> The **www.LakeLucerne.ch** website lists the numerous ferry trip, combination packages and tour options available. Tickets may be purchased directly from this site.

- Day Tickets / Passes: Purchase a one-day pass that allows you to use the ferries to all Lake Lucerne destinations. It may be used as a "hop-on/hop-off" service and you may make last minute changes in plans. An unlimited number of trips may be taken during the designated day with one of these passes. Substantial savings vs the cost of individual trip tickets may be realized if you are taking multiple trips in one day.

- Discounts are available for children.

Family Day Tickets: This is an interesting choice for families who are visiting the area. The Family Day Ticket is good for unlimited travel for a full day on the ferries. Some details and limitations include:

> **Family Day Tickets**
>
> A good option for families who will be using the ferry system is the Family Day Tickets. One flat rate covers the family.

- Limited to 2nd class.

- Must be at least one adult and no more than two adults.

- A maximum of four children are included in the pass and must be a maximum of 16 years old.

Lake & Mountain Combination Tickets: If you plan on combining your ferry trip with a mountain adventure, check with the tourist office for options available. Most gondola or cogwheel rides from towns which border the lake provide the ability to purchase a discounted ferry/mountain adventure.

Examples of Combination Tickets include:

o   Mount Klewenalp – from Beckenried

o   Mount Rigi – from Vitznau or Weggis

o   Mount Pilatus Silver or Golden Round Trip

o   Bürgenstock catamaran and funicular

Ticket Classes: Most ferry routes provide 1st and 2nd class seating.

- The cost for 1st class tickets and passes is typically around 150% of a 2nd class ticket.

- 2nd class tickets may be upgraded while en route.

- 1st class tickets enable you to travel on the upper deck(s). 2nd class tickets require you to remain on the lower deck. Both decks provide the ability to step out into the air and take great photographs.

- 2nd class decks are often more crowded.

- Both decks provide the ability to purchase snacks.

Purchasing Tickets: Tickets, including single-trip, day passes and combination trips, may be purchased from several locations.

- Ferry ticket office at Pier 1 in Lucerne and in Weggis

- Tourist office in the train station.

- Purchase onboard the vessel from the ticket dispenser near where you board.

- Online from: shop.LakeLucerne.ch

Multiple Stops: The further a destination is from Lucerne, the greater the likelihood of the ferry making stops along the way. For example, most trips to Beckenried make 3 or four stops en route. Trips to Vitznau make at least 1 stop before reaching Vitznau.

Restrooms: All ferries have restrooms on board. There is no charge to use these facilities.

Dogs and Bikes: Bicycles can be brought aboard for no additional fee. Dogs are allowed on non-culinary (lunch or dinner) cruises. There is an extra fee to bring a dog.

Handicapped Accessible: All ferries will accommodate wheelchairs.

Lake Cruises: Perhaps you don't wish to head off to another town but still want to experience these delightful ferries. A good solution is to hop onto one of the many short excursions. Example tours include:

> Caution: During the busy summer season, several of these cruises fill up quickly. Book ahead if you can.

- Short Cruise – travel to Beckenried and return. Duration is 2.5 hours.

- Bürgenstock Short Cruise – round trip to Kehristen-Bürgenstock from Lucerne on a unique catamaran. One hour duration.

- Grand Lake Cruise – spend over five hours cruising most of Lake Lucerne on this round-trip event. Travel to the town of Flüehen at the far end of Lake Lucerne. Duration is five and ½ hours.

- Cruises from Weggis: Several excursions also depart out of Weggis. A fun addition if you will be staying in the lovely small town.

- Culinary Cruises: Cruises from Lucerne which provide meals are, in the high season, available for most meals including breakfast, lunch and dinner. A great way to enjoy a meal.

~ ~ ~ ~ ~

8: Lake Lucerne Towns to Explore

Visiting one of the villages or small towns along Lake Lucerne provides an added dimension to your understanding and appreciation of this area. Switzerland is not just all about its cities and mountains, rather, the many towns which are not tourist hot spots are a great way to experience what living in Switzerland is like.

Recommended Lake Lucerne Towns:

The following map and pages outline five communities which are enjoyable and relaxing destinations. Consider traveling to one of these sites either just for a relaxing day trip or to stay in lodging for your visit to the Lucerne area.

In each case, these communities provide:

- Easy access by multiple modes of transportation from Lucerne and reachable in under 90 minutes. Most are reachable in under one hour.

- Restaurants, lodgings, and shops near the ferry stop.

- Delightful architecture and views.

- Most of these towns also have easy access to mountain destinations.

- Minimal crowds when compared to Lucerne.

Lodging Suggestion

Consider booking your lodging in one of the lakeshore towns instead of Lucerne. Costs are often less with far smaller crowds and easier access to nature.

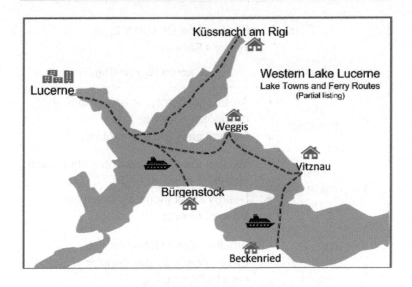

Five Great Lakeside Destinations
Author's Ranking

Rank	Location	Reason for Ranking
1	Weggis	• Beautiful small town with great browsing, views, mountain access, and park along the lake. • Easy access by ferry from Lucerne.
2	Vitznau	• Attractive village with only moderate tourism. • Easy access to Mt Rigi. • Lakeside restaurants and lodging.
3	Bür-genstock	• Closest to Lucerne of the 5 destinations listed here.

Five Great Lakeside Destinations Author's Ranking		
Rank	**Location**	**Reason for Ranking**
3	Bür- genstock	• An upscale array of hotels and shops overlooking the lake. • Several easy trails to explore.
4	Küss- nacht am Rigi	• Midsize town with attractive shops and streets to browse. • Nearby small mountain to explore. • Minimal crowds.
5	Becken- ried	• Small village with few tourists. • Easy access to the popular mountain resort of Klewenalp. • Little in town to explore.

1 - Weggis:

General Description: Weggis is a popular small town with a pop- ulation near 4,400. The size allows for this town to have most of the normal desired amenities while not giving the feeling of being in a busy city. If you have time to visit only one Switzerland village outside of Lucerne, you can't go wrong in selecting Weggis.

Weggis has much to offer to visitors.

• Easy to reach by ferry from Lucerne.
• Good opportunities for browsing, sightseeing, and shopping.
• While appealing to tourists, the crowds are nowhere near the volume of Lucerne.
• Gondola to Mount Rigi.
• Many lodging options.

The town of Weggis
At the foot of Mount Rigi

This is a popular jumping-off spot for visiting Mt. Rigi. A gondola departs from a station which is a bit uphill from the ferry dock and may be a challenge to some. If you are coming to Weggis by ferry, an extra transportation component of a taxi or shuttle (when available) may be appropriate to reach the gondola.

Location: Weggis is on the northern shore of Lake Lucerne and northeast of Lucerne city. It is at the base of Mt. Rigi.

Travel to Weggis: This town may be reached from Lucerne by car, ferry, or a bus-train combination.

- Ferry: Travel time from Lucerne is roughly 45 minutes with several ferries departing each day. The Weggis ferry terminal is next to the tourist center which can provide mountain transportation, and tour tickets. Several shops, restaurants, and inns are close to the terminal.

- Train-Bus Combo. Taking a train from Lucerne requires switching to a bus at the Küssnacht train station. This train-bus combo operates about one per hour and travel time is roughly 50 minutes each way. The bus will drop you off near the ferry terminal in the heart of the tourist area.

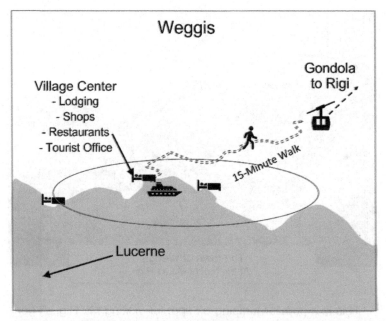

Mountain adventures available: Mount Rigi is accessible from Weggis by a combination of a gondola for the first part of the trip and then change mid-way to a cogwheel train.

Lodging in Town: This location has more lodging than the other communities on this list. Several, such as the Post Hotel, are near the ferry terminal. Others, such as the Hotel Central and See Hotel are a few blocks walk.

Some Weggis lodging options include:

- <u>Beauge Rivage</u>: An attractive and slightly upscale, small hotel about 2 blocks from the ferry terminal. 4-stars. www.Beaurivage-Weggis.ch

- <u>Post Hotel Weggis</u>: Very close to the ferry terminal. 4-stars. Great views of the lake and several restaurants nearby. www.Post-Hotel-Weggis.ch

- <u>Frohburg:</u> Relaxed property with great views. About 1 block from ferry terminal. Mid-Priced. 4-stars. www.Frohburg.ch.

2 - Vitznau:

General Description: Vitznau, a charming village of 1,400 people, has been a popular resort destination for hundreds of years. A driver of the town's popularity is the large spa hotel "The Park Hotel Vitznau." This property which sits on the western edge of Vitznau has often been a retreat for royalty and celebrities.

Vitznau is a charming small town tucked up against steep mountains.

Vitznau offers more than one large and expensive spa. It is a small but appealing village to visit and stay in. It lies at the base of Rigi, and a cogwheel train takes visitors to and from the mountain. When visiting here, there are several blocks of shops, restaurants, and inns to visit. Views south toward the Alps are spectacular.

Negatives to visiting here are few. The small size of this community and lack of crowds will be a positive or negative depending on your preferences. If you choose to stay here, lodging can be expensive.

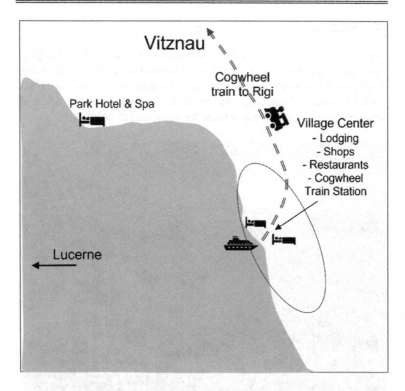

Location: Vitznau is east of Lucerne and sits along the northern shore of Lake Lucerne. It is at the base of Mount Rigi which is easily accessible by cogwheel train.

Travel to Vitznau: This town is easily reached by ferry or bus. Trains, with the exception of the cogwheel train, do not service this village.

- <u>Ferry</u>: Travel time from Lucerne is roughly one hour. The ferry station is immediately adjacent to the cogwheel train terminal. Several shops, restaurants, and inns are close to the terminal. Vitznau is a popular destination and ferries run frequently with more operating in the spring and summer. Check Rome2rio.com for the schedule.

- <u>Train-Bus Combo.</u> Taking a train from Lucerne requires switching to a bus at the Küssnacht train station. This train-

94

bus combo operates roughly one per hour and travel time is about the same as taking the ferry. The bus will drop you off near the ferry terminal. It also stops at the famed Park Hotel, should you decide to stay there.

Mountain Adventures Available: Mount Rigi is easily accessible from Vitznau Küssnacht by a fun cogwheel train which departs from the center of town.

Lodging in Town: In addition to the noted Park Hotel Vitznau, there are several small hotels near the ferry and cogwheel train terminal.

Vitznau's upscale Park Hotel is stunning. If you have a large budget, it is a great place to stay.
Photo Source: Lkiwaner - Wikimedia Commons

- Hotel Rigi Vitznau – 4-star. On the main street a short walk up from the terminal. www.Rigi-Vitznau.ch.

- Hotel Terrasse am See – 3.5-star. Immediately on the water, and next to the ferry terminal. www.Hotel-Terrasse.ch

- <u>Neuro Campus Hotel</u> – 4-star. Newer, fairly modern, hotel, rooms with large balconies. Moderately priced. Close to ferry and cogwheel train. <u>www.DasMorgen.ch</u>

- <u>Hotel Vitznauerrhof</u> – 4.5 stars. Classic, somewhat upscale hotel on the water and just one block from the ferry and cogwheel train. <u>www.Vitznauerhof.ch.</u>

- <u>Park Hotel Vitznau</u> – 5 stars. Upscale, full-service hotel and spa. Pricey. The only downside, other than price, is the distance from central Vitznau. <u>www.ParkHotel-Vitznau.ch</u>

3 -Bürgenstock:

General Description: This destination differs from the others on this list. Instead of arriving at a lakeside town, you arrive at a small dock (if you come by ferry) and are immediately whisked uphill to a resort complex which sits high on the cliffs above the lake.

Bürgenstock Resort
Two of the four hotels at the resort.

Bürgenstock was also described in chapter 6 on mountain adventures. This can either be an easy day trip from Lucerne or a great place to stay. Visitors here are not all guests of the hotel complex as many people travel here for an enjoyable few hours to explore the resort, views and trails.

When visiting here for just a day, cost is not generally an issue although the restaurants are pricey. If you choose to stay in one of the properties' hotels, be prepared to encounter higher prices than found in Lucerne City.

Location: southeast of Lucerne on a high bluff overlooking the southern shore.

Travel to Bürgenstock: This resort is best reached by ferry or car. Taking a ferry is recommended. The ferry stop is "Kehrsiten-Bürgenstock." Travel time for either car or ferry is approximately 25 minutes each way.

Bürgenstock Ferry
Unique modern catamaran which services only
Bürgenstock from Lucerne.

When arriving by ferry, there is a connection to a funicular in the same building. The funicular takes visitors up to the lodge in a short but enjoyable journey.

Lodging at the resort: Four hotels are open, and all are upscale with differing levels of amenities and restaurants. Full details on Bürgenstock lodging may be found at: **www.BurgenstockResort.com.**

4-Küssnacht am Rigi: (Often cited simply as Küssnacht)

General Description: This is the largest town in this list. With a population of over 13,000, Küssnacht am Rigi has a lot to offer visitors including a pedestrian mall, numerous shops, broad lakeside boulevards, and boutique hotels.

Küssnacht is nestled in a valley which borders Lake Lucerne and is close to the large Lake Zug to the north. To the east and west, Küssnacht is framed by mountains, with the popular Mount Rigi situated along the town's east side.

> **William Tell**
> Fun fact – Küssnacht is where the William Tell episode took place in the 14th century.

Unlike the other communities listed here, there is no immediate connection to a major mountain resort or ski area. It is, however, a fairly short trip to reach Mount Rigi.

Location: This is the northernmost town on Lake Lucerne. It sits at the top of a large northeast tip of a long northward arm of the lake.

Travel to Küssnacht am Rigi: This town is easily reached by ferry, bus, or train.

- Ferry: Travel time from Lucerne is roughly 50 minutes. The ferry station is close to the heart of the town's central shopping district. Note, the ferry does make stops en route to Lucerne. Ferry trips are limited with more running in the spring and summer than in winter. Check Rome2rio.com for current schedule.

- Train: Numerous trains per day which take only 20 minutes from Lucerne. The train station in Küssnacht is away from the town center and necessitates a 10-15-minute walk along busy streets, or you can take a taxi.

- <u>Bus.</u> Taking a bus between Küssnacht and Lucerne is often the quickest way to travel. Travel time of 24 minutes is like taking the train, but the bus stop at "Küssnacht am Rigi Plaza" takes you close to the heart of town. Buses run at least one per hour during the day.

The town of Küsnacht am Rigi.
Photo Source: Chrisaliv - Wikimedia Commons

Mountain Adventures Available: Seebodenalp, a lowkey resort area with overlooks, hotel, numerous hiking trails, and winter sports opportunities. Easily reached by gondola from Küssnacht am Rigi. Mount Rigi may be reached by taking a 15-minute bus ride to Weggis or Arth-Goldau.

Lodging in Town: The following establishments are near the ferry terminal and central Küssnacht:

- <u>Hotel-Restaurant Seehof</u> – 3.5-star hotel and restaurant on the lake next to the ferry dock. <u>www.Hotel-Restaurant-See-hof.ch.</u>

- <u>Hotel-Zum-Hirschen</u> – 3-star small inn in the heart of town. <u>www.HirschenRestaurant.ch</u>
- <u>Bahnhoefli</u> – 3.5-star B & B situated near the train station. Outdoor dining and old Swiss charm. <u>www.Bahnhoefli-Kuessnacht.ch</u>

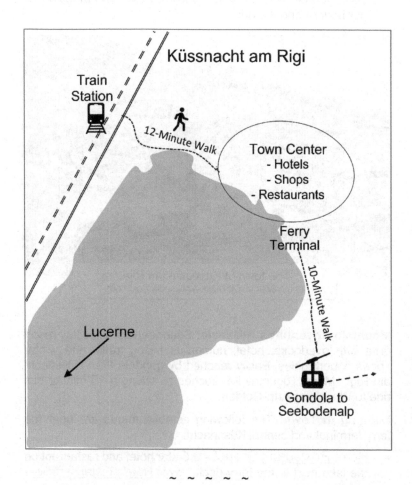

5- Beckenried:

The attractive village of Beckenried

General Description: Small community of 3,500 which provides a quiet stay. This is a long and narrow village with most buildings along the lakeside. This is a relaxed village with minimal tourist crowds and easy access to the Klewenalp ski area.

Once here, there is not a lot to explore. Come here for the ease of access to the neighboring ski area and the ability to enjoy a small Swiss town. It is the furthest from Lucerne of the five communities recommended in this guide. As a result of this distance, travel time is a little longer.

Location: southeast of Lucerne on the southern shore.

Travel to Beckenried: Ferry, car, or train and bus combo may be taken. The ferry time is slightly over one hour. To reach here by train from Lucerne, a train and bus combination is required. This train and bus combo takes under one hour each way.

<u>Important ferry note:</u> There are two ferry terminals in Beckenried. Knowing which one you are heading to can be helpful when

planning your trip. If you are traveling from Lucerne, all ferries carry only passengers and take you to the main ferry stop near where the cogwheel train departs. If you are coming from Gersau, this is a car and passenger ferry and lands at the "Beckenried-Niederdorf" ferry terminal slightly west of central Beckenried.

Mountain Adventures Available: Klewenalp ski area via gondola from Beckenried. This gondola is a short 5-minute ride from the main ferry terminal.

Lodging in Town: The following are near the ferry terminal and nearby restaurants. Only the hotels within a short distance from the ferry and gondola are listed. Other hotels are in town but not within easy walking distance.

- Hotel Nidwaldnerhof – 4-star hotel. www.Nidwaldnerhof.ch. 6-minute walk to ferry terminal.

- Hotel-Restaurant Rössli – 3-star small inn. Immediately next to the ferry terminal. www.Roessli-Beckenried.ch

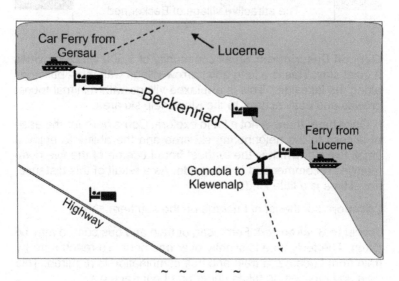

9: Where to Stay in the Lucerne Area

Where you choose to stay when visiting a new city is essentially a personal choice. You may prefer hotels or rental apartments. Picking a place guided by your budget may be critical to you.

Regardless of the motives which drive your selection of accommodation type, the "where in town should I stay?" question is critical to helping you have an enjoyable visit.

> **Good News...**
>
> Every area of Lucerne can offer a good night's stay and quality lodging.

In addition to in-town lodging, the Lucerne area provides enjoyable lodging out of town. With many cities, picking a hotel or B & B 30-45 minutes out of town might not be appealing, with Lucerne, just the opposite can be true as these out-of-town areas can actually enhance your experience.

There are essentially 3 broad categories of areas to consider for lodging:

- In Lucerne City
- Lakeside communities
- Mountain lodging and resorts

This guide does not provide details on all hotels in Lucerne as there are simply too many to describe. There are many fine and dynamic online sources such as Trip Advisor or Hotels.com and others which provide far more detail than can be provided here. These sites will include answers to every question on a property you are considering and allow you to make reservations once you have made your selection.

Staying in Lucerne City:

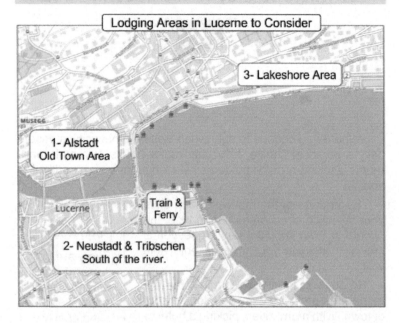

Lodging Areas in Lucerne to Consider

3- Lakeshore Area

1- Alstadt
Old Town Area

Train &
Ferry

2- Neustadt & Tribschen
South of the river.

Three Areas in Lucerne to Consider: Following are descriptions of three sections of town with a good variety of lodging in areas which are recommended.

Altstadt – Old Town Section of Lucerne:

Staying here puts you in the heart of it all. Old Town is where most first-time visitors go and for good reason. This is a charming section of town with many historical buildings and easy access to museums, the river, numerous shops, and restaurants.

There is a good range of lodging to consider. Some of the properties are situated directly on the river, providing excellent views from your room.

Distance from any part of this historical center to the main train and ferry stations is less than a 10-minute walk.

Hotel des Balances
One of the hotels overlooking the Reuss River from Old Town.

The largest negative often experienced here is noise. Being right in the center of the tourist area, it is natural to encounter noise throughout the day and well into the evening. This is especially the case if you like to open a window in your room.

Old Town/Altstadt Lodging to Consider:

- Hotel Pickwick: Directly overlooks the Reuss River and the Chapel Bridge. 4-Star. Mid-priced. www.HotelPickwick.ch.

- Des Alpes: Also overlooks the Chapel Bridge. 3.5-stars. Mid-priced. www.Desalpes-Luzern.ch

- Hotel des Balances: Overlooks the Reuss River and is a bit away from the crowds visiting the Chapel Bridge. Higher priced rooms. 5-star. www.Balances.ch.

- Hotel Magic Luzern: One block from the river and facing a small plaza. 3.5 stars. www.Magic-Hotel.ch

- Alstadt Hotel La Stelle Luzern: Boutique, small property in the heart of Old Town. 3.5 stars. www.Lestelle.ch

Neustadt (New Town) & Tribschen District of Lucerne:

The areas south of the river, across from Old Town are away from the tourist center while still providing ease of access to many attractions. Hotels here are close to the main train and ferry stations, which can be helpful if you will be taking day trips. This section spans a long narrow area ranging from the Spreuer Bridge to a short distance beyond the train station.

Radisson Blu Hotel
Modern luxury - very close to the train station.
Photo Source: Radisson Blu

The negatives of staying here are the lack of views which many properties in the other areas can provide. It is also a greater walk to such attractions as the Lion Monument and Glacier Garden.

Cost for lodging here varies greatly as the properties range from small, lowkey hotels such as Hotel Central to larger, more notable properties like the Renaissance Lucerne.

If you wish a quiet respite from the crowded tourist sections, but still want reasonable access to most attractions, this area should be considered. Another benefit here are the small grocery stores which can come in handy. The largest grocery is, surprisingly, located in the lower level of the train station.

New Town Lodging to Consider:

- Hotel Central Luzern: Small hotel on a quiet side street. 3.5 stars. Mid-priced. www.Hotel-Central-Luzern.com.

- Ameron Luzern Hotel Flora: 4 stars. Boutique property on a side street which is very convenient to the train station and Chapel Bridge. www.AmeronHotels.com

- Renaissance Lucerne Hotel: Large hotel with full range of amenities. Part of Marriott chain. 4.5 stars. www.Marriott.com.

- Radisson Blu Hotel Lucerne: Large hotel located near the train and ferry stations. On the far side of the train station which sets it outside of the main New Town area. 4 stars. www.RadissonHotels.com

- Wilden Mann: Boutique hotel situated on a quiet pedestrian street with several shops and restaurants. Close to the river, but further from the train station than most other properties in the area. 4-star. Mid to high priced. www.Wilden-Mann.ch.

- Hotel Monopol Luzern: Large, ornate hotel situated next to the main train and ferry stations. 4-star. Mid-to high price range. www.MonopolLuzern.ch.

~ ~ ~ ~ ~ ~

Lakeshore (Northern shore) Near Town:

Several of Lucerne's most historic and notable hotel properties may be found along the stretch of lake immediately east from Old Town. Lodging here is often more expensive and upscale but for good reason. The views of the lake and town from hotels such as Grand National or Art Deco Hotel Montana are superb.

Grand National Hotel
Historic, 5-star+ luxury hotel overlooking Lake Lucerne.

In addition to the upscale properties, several smaller hotels and inns may be found closer to the historical center and near the St. Leodegar Church. Views from many of these hotels are superb and the quality of service in several, such as the Grand National or Mandarin Oriental Palace can't be beat.

This section of Lucerne may have a few downsides. There is a greater walking distance to the main ferry and train stations than from other areas of town. Inns closer to Old Town will incur more tourist traffic with increased likelihood of noise.

Lakeshore Area Lodging to Consider:

- <u>Grand Hotel National Luzern</u>: Upscale, historic, and large property overlooking the lake. 5-stars. Pricey but superb service. <u>www.Grandhotel-national.com</u>

- <u>Mandarin Oriental Palace, Luzern</u>: Another high-end, 5-star hotel well worth considering. A bit further from town center but some reduction in tourist crowds. <u>www.MandarinOriental.com</u>

- <u>Hotel Hofgarten</u>: Boutique lodging near St. Leodegar Church and close to Old Town. 4-star. Mid-range pricing. <u>www.Hofgarten.ch.</u>

- <u>Art Deco Hotel Montana</u>: Upscale hotel, situated slightly uphill to provide great views of the city and lake. 5-star. Mid-to-high priced. <u>www.Hotel-Montana.ch</u>.

Staying in a Lakeside Community:

Chapter 8 provided an overview of several villages and towns along the shores of Lake Lucerne. These locations provide a pleasant alternative for lodging in lieu of staying in the heart of Lucerne City.

Choosing one of the highlighted communities vs. staying in Lucerne provides several advantages and disadvantages:

- **Tourist Crowds:** Lakeside communities offer an advantage here. Getting away from Lucerne greatly reduces the volume of tourist crowds, tour groups, and buses you will encounter.

- **Train Travel:** There is an advantage to staying in Lucerne if you are likely to take several train trips up to a variety of nearby mountains or towns. If, however, your plans do not include multiple train trips, then consider staying in one of the lakeside villages.

- **Exploring Lucerne:** When staying in communities such as Weggis or Bürgenstock, it is easy and fun to commute into Lucerne for a day of exploration. Staying in either Lucerne or a lakeside resort provides an ability to explore all that Lucerne has to offer.

- **Mountain Explorations:** Staying in a lakeside village provides the ability to easily explore <u>one</u>, but usually only one, mountain resort. The feature of having a gondola or cogwheel train within walking distance of your lodging can be fun, especially if you plan on taking several hikes or putting in days of winter sports.

  The tradeoff is when staying in Lucerne, it is easy to have day trips to many different mountains, but only after traveling some distance to reach them.

Staying on a Mountain:

Most of the mountain resorts and recreation areas around Lucerne provide lodging. Chapter 6 recommends several mountain areas to visit, and the lodging will range from small backpacker inns to luxury hotels. Some lodges, such as the one on Mt. Pilatus

Pilatus Kulm Hotel
Mountain hotel near the peak of Pilatus with incredible views from most rooms.

offer special nighttime activities such as stargazing from small observatories.

Bürgenstock: Four different lodging options ranging from the rustic Taverne 1879 to the luxury Palace Hotel. Most are expensive with great views of the lake below. www.BurgenstockResort.com.

Klewenalp: Midsize, rustic mountain inn with easy access to ski and hiking trails and lifts. Low to mid-range pricing. www.Klewennalp.com

Pilatus: Two small hotels, the Hotel Bellevue and Hotel Pilatus-Kulm. Both with incredible mountain and panoramic views. Mid-priced. Star gazing is provided during some evenings. www.Pilatus.ch.

Rigi: Several lodging opportunities including mountain homes and inns. Check the Rigi website to explore the options. Lodging is situated at several levels from midway up the mountain to the top. www.Rigi.ch.

Stoos: Similar to Rigi, the Stoos mountain area has several places to stay, and they include hotels, holiday homes, and rustic ski lodges. The accommodations page on the Stoos-Muotatal website provides details on each of the properties. www.Stoos-Muotatal.ch

~ ~ ~ ~ ~ ~

Appendix: Helpful Online References

To help you expand your knowledge of this area, several online reference sites are listed here. Lucerne and the Lake Lucerne area is popular so there is a wealth of online material which can help in planning your trip.

Following is a list of online references to this city and area. The purpose of this list is to enhance your understanding of what is available before embarking on your trip. Any online search will result in the websites outlined here plus many others. These are listed as they are professionally done, and most do not only try to sell you tours.

I.	Travel Cards and Passes
Card or Pass	**Website address and description**
Lucerne Visitor Card	Provided free to overnight guests at Lucerne area hotels. Details are provided on all locations accepting the Visitor Card. - **www.Luzern.com**
Museum Pass	Two variations, the Lucerne Museum Pass and the Swiss Museum Pass. - **www.MuseumPass.ch**

I.	Travel Cards and Passes
Card or Pass	**Website address and description**
Swiss Coupon Pass	May be purchased separately or obtain at no extra cost as part of the Swiss Travel Pass. - **www.Swiss-Pass.ch**
Swiss Travel Pass	Popular travel pass which covers most public transportation and many mountain adventures. - **www.Swiss-Pass.ch**
Tell-Pass	Travel and coupon pass for central Switzerland which includes Lucerne. - **www.TellPass.ch**

II.	Lucerne and Switzerland City Info
Website Name or Type	**Website**
Lucerne Visitor Center website	- Overview of what is available in Lucerne, events, tours, where to stay, mountain excursions and more. - Details at the Lucerne Tourist Information office. - **www.Luzern.com**
My Switzerland	Good information on all aspects of traveling to Switzerland. Numerous links take the user to specific websites for attractions, passes, tours, hotels and more. - **www.MySwitzerland.com**

II.	Lucerne and Switzerland City Info
Website Name or Type	**Website**
Lucerne Events	The following websites provide details on some of the more popular events held each year in Lucerne. - Blue Balls Festival – **www.Blue-Balls.ch** - Lucerne Festival – **www.LucerneFestival.ch**
Switzerland Travel Center	- Details on passes, tours, and transportation available in Switzerland. - **www.SwitzerlandTravelCentre.com**

III.	Lucerne Museums and Attractions
Museum or Attraction	**Website**
My Swiss Alps	- Good overview of most attractions and tours around Lucerne and other towns. Tickets may be purchased from this site. - **www.MySwissAlps.com**
Lucerne Museums website	- Information and passes for all area museums. - **www.MuseenLuzern.ch**
Alpineum	- Collection of large diorama paintings, models of Swiss houses and railroads. - **Alpineum.ch**

III. Lucerne Museums and Attractions	
Museum or Attraction	**Website**
Bourbaki Panorama	- Circular diorama focusing on elements of Swiss history. - **www.BourbakiPanorama.ch**
Glacier Gardens	- Glacial features, fossils, and museum. - **www.GlacierGarden.ch**
Musegg Wall and Fortifications	- Long wall with fortifications and towers bordering Lucerne's Old Town. - **www.Museggmauer.ch**
Museum Sammlung Rosengart	- Art museum with large collection of contemporary and modern art. - **www.Rosengart.ch**
Swiss Museum of Transport	- Expansive transportation museum covering air, rail, auto, and water. - **www.Verkehrshaus.ch**

IV. Area Mountains	
Mountain Area	**Website address and description**
All Swiss Mountains	- Website detailing most Swiss mountains, ski areas, and resorts. - **www.MySwissAlps.com**
My Switzerland	- Good overview of most mountain adventures, lodging, travel, and tours throughout Switzerland. - **www.MySwitzerland.com**

IV. Area Mountains	
Mountain Area	**Website address and description**
Bürgenstock Resort	- Upscale resort and alpine area. - www.BurgenstockResort.com
Klewenalp	- Ski area with numerous trails for summer and winter activities. - www.Klewenalp.ch
Pilatus	- Popular mountain adventure and cogwheel train close to Lucerne. - www.Pilatus.ch
Rigi	- Mountain resort and hiking area situated just north of Lake Lucerne. - www.Rigi.ch
Stanserhorn	- Popular ski and winter sports area. - www.Stanserhorn.ch
Stoos and Fronalpstock	- Mountain village with the world's steepest funicular leading to it. Located on the eastern side of Lake Lucerne. - www.Stoos-Muotatal.ch
Titlis	- Popular tall peak south of Lucerne with great views and several activities to consider. - www.Titlis.ch

V.	Transportation Information and Tickets
Website Name or Type	**Website Address & Description**
Lake Lucerne Ferries	- Ferry system with numerous routes which cover most lakeside towns and villages. - www.LakeLucerne.ch
My Swiss Alps	- Information and time schedules for ferries, buses, and local trains. - www.MySwissAlps.com
Rome2rio	Excellent site to find travel time, costs, and schedules for travel within Europe for: driving, ferries, trains, taxi. - www.Rome2rio.com
Train Ticket Resellers	Several services enable you to purchase train tickets online prior to your trip, including: - RailEurope.com - TrainLine.com - Eurorailways.com These sites are a good place to check schedules and train availability for all train companies servicing most areas in Europe.
Bus Travel and Tickets	Several online sites provide ability to search Switzerland area bus schedules and purchase tickets online: - BusBud.com - FlixBus.com - Rome2rio.com

VI.	General Tour and Hotel Booking Sites
Company	**Website address and description**
Hotel Sites	Numerous online sites enable you to review and book hotels online. Most of these sites also resell tours. - **Booking.com** - **Hotels.com** - **Expedia.com** - **Travelocity.com**
Tour Resellers	Many companies, such as the ones listed here, provide a full variety of tours to Lucerne as well as day tours. The offerings are similar, but research is helpful as some firms offer unique services and tours. - **GetYourGuide.com** - **ToursByLocals.com** - **Viator.com**
Trip Advisor	**www.TripAdvisor.com** One of the most comprehensive sites on hotels and tours. Direct connection with Viator, a tour reseller.

Index

Starting-Point Travel Guides

This guidebook on Lucerne is one of several current and planned *Starting-Point Guides*. Each book in the series is developed with the concept of using one enjoyable city as your basecamp and then exploring from there.

Current guidebooks are for:

Austria:

- Salzburg, and the Salzburg area.

France:

- Bordeaux, Plus the surrounding Gironde River region
- Dijon Plus the Burgundy Region
- Lille and the Nord-Pas-de-Calais Area.
- Nantes and the western Loire Valley.
- Reims and Épernay the heart of the Champagne Region.
- Strasbourg, and the central Alsace region.
- Toulouse, and the Haute-Garonne area.

Germany:

- Cologne & Bonn
- Dresden and the Saxony State
- Stuttgart and the and the Baden-Württemberg area.

Spain:

- Camino Easy: A mature walker's guide to the popular Camino de Santiago trail.
- Toledo: The City of Three Cultures

Sweden:

- <u>Gothenburg</u> Plus the Västra Götaland region.

Switzerland:

- <u>Geneva</u>, Including the Lake Geneva area.
- <u>Lucerne</u>, Including the Lake Lucerne area.
- <u>Zurich</u> – And the Lake Zurich area.

Updates on these and other titles may be found on the author's Facebook page at:

www.Facebook.com/BGPreston.author

Feel free to use this Facebook page to provide feedback and suggestions to the author or email to: cincy3@gmail.com

Made in United States
Orlando, FL
06 November 2024

53536274R00075